BRIGHT IDEAS

M… the most of …useum visits

Written by Gail Durbin and Susan Morris

Published by Scholastic Ltd,
Villiers House,
Clarendon Avenue,
Leamington Spa,
Warwickshire CV32 5PR

1 2 3 4 5 6 7 8 9 0 6 7 8 9 0 1 2 3 4 5
Authors Gail Durbin and Susan Morris
Editor Libby Weaver
Designer Claire Belcher
Illustrations by Jane Bottomley
Cover design by Sue Stockbridge
Cover photograph by Martyn Chillmaid
Designed using Aldus Pagemaker
Printed in Great Britain by Clays Ltd, Suffolk

The authors would like to thank colleagues they have worked with over the years whose ideas they have drawn on. They would particularly like to thank Carole Mahoney and Mark Eller for help while the book was in production.

British Library Cataloguing-in-Publication Data
A catalogue record for this book is available from the British Library

ISBN 0-590-53574-9

Contents

Introduction

Museums in Britain are a rich and ever-growing resource. A visit to a museum (we use the term 'museum' in this book to include gallery, historic house or site) can be one of the most exciting and memorable parts of a child's primary education. In this book we provide a range of activities both to focus pupils' interest and to give you alternatives to worksheets.

HOW TO USE THIS BOOK

The activity ideas are grouped according to the type of collections commonly found in museums. Methods are intended to be transferable however, so that you could take activities from one section and apply them to a different type of collection from the one suggested. You are not obliged to have all the children in a class do the same activity: you can choose to have different groups tackling different tasks simultaneously, which has the benefit of avoiding overcrowding round some exhibits.

PREPARING FOR THE VISIT

In museums children can learn about the world by examining objects and material evidence. If you are planning to take your class to a museum therefore, you would do well to give children some advance practice in the techniques which will help. This will allow them to unlock the excitement and interest from the objects for themselves and become independent learners. It will also avoid you having to be an expert who knows all about, say, Bronze Age axes, so that you can tell them 'the facts'; if children can analyse the objects, they will find out some of what they need to know for themselves. Pre-eminent among these necessary skills is the need for slow, careful observation and, following closely on, the need to record what has been observed. We have provided a number of activities to help develop these skills and strongly recommend that you build some of them in before any visit. Once learned, they are transferable to other areas right across the curriculum and will not be wasted.

WHICH MUSEUM IS BEST?

The temptation is often to plan a big day out to a large national museum some distance away. This will provide a very exciting but also exhausting day for the children and yourself. Do not overlook your local museum. There are many benefits of staying closer to home even for older pupils. The atmosphere may be quieter and friendlier, the liaison more personal, and the children will gain useful knowledge about what is available to them locally. Displays may be smaller, but most activities in this book show how you only need a few well-chosen items to make a focused, doable activity which the children will enjoy. One of the hoped-for results of a visit should be that children will want to visit museums in the future, and they are more likely to want to do this if the experience is pleasant.

WHEN SHOULD YOU VISIT A MUSEUM?

It is better *not* to go at the absolute end of a topic, when there will be no lesson time left to use the information or ideas gained. Otherwise, you could go equally well towards the beginning, middle or end of your term's work. What is important, however, is using the visit to achieve a well-defined purpose and tying it firmly into the children's work rather than creating an isolated experience. At the beginning of a term's work on water, for instance, you might want to do a survey of how boats or fish are shaped to float and move in water, in order to organise subsequent experiments with models in school. Towards the end of a term in which you studied the Romans, you might need to find out exactly how mosaics were made so that a classroom mosaic summarising what you have discovered about life in Roman times can be made.

If you intend to go out for a whole day, consider varying activities so that the ones requiring a lot of mental effort take place in the morning, while the ones requiring less effort or a higher level of physical activity take place in the afternoon.

THE VISIT AS AN ESSENTIAL STEP

At whatever stage of the term's work you are, ideally you want your children to feel that the only way to accomplish the next step is to visit the museum and obtain what they need.

You may need to stage-manage this a little, but getting children to express voluntarily their 'need' to visit is very valuable. It will help you if the children have shared in identifying the objectives and planned outcomes of the visit. Over-extended aims or unfocused on-site tasks can be eliminated. It also means that when the children arrive in the museum they are already motivated, independent researchers, ready to go, and clear about their purpose, not passively waiting to go through the motions of some task.

Children can participate to the full in the pattern of preparation, visit and follow-up. Their work after the museum visit will be much more inventive and penetrating than just writing up an account of the day. They can know in advance that the destination of the material they record on the visit is its use in a design, a computer program, a wall-hanging, a piece of expressive writing, a role-play, a scientific experiment, an assembly, a table-display or whatever.

INVOLVING CHILDREN IN PLANNING THE PRACTICALITIES

There are invaluable benefits to be gained by involving pupils in the planning aspects of the visit such as the timetable or the transport from the very start. It helps ensure that they are very committed to the main purpose of the visit (rather than just the packed lunch!) and can pace themselves instead of becoming exhausted by the initial excitement. On their return, it also gives them a sense of personal achievement and success which is very important for developing their confidence for visiting such places again individually or with their families.

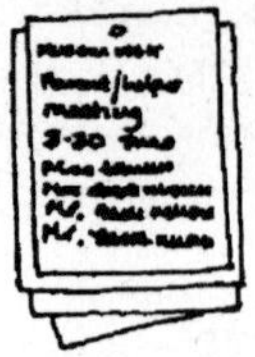

ESSENTIAL CHECKLIST OF PRE-VISIT PLANNING

- Preliminary visit to museum to check what is on show and plan activity
- Obtain permission of head
- Obtain permission of parents
- Arrange cover if needed
- Book with museum*
- Book transport
- Notify school kitchens about lunch arrangements
- Prepare or collect materials and activity sheets
- Hold pre-visit meeting to brief adults who will accompany you
- Plan how to evaluate visit afterwards.

*Remember, *you must book in advance* with the museum, even if you are not using their education staff. It is your only way of finding out for sure whether the objects you want to see will be on show, and alerting the museum to what you need. A display which is open the day you do your preliminary visit may be closed the next day!

EXTRA ADULTS AS SUPERVISORS

For the teacher, one of the most invaluable assets on any visit out of school can be the accompanying adults: extra hands, extra supervision and advice at moments of need! However, from these adults' point of view, the visit can be a worrying experience if they are not sure what you expect, or a boring one if they are only used as escorts.

Try to provide them with an opportunity to meet you in advance, talk to them on the coach or put some guidelines on paper. Ideally you should go through the timetable, meeting points, standards of expected behaviour and so on, as these will loom large in their minds. More importantly, however, talk about the purpose of the visit (the educational activity) so that they can share in this too. Make sure that they are clear what the aim of the task is, the sort of exhibits they will use, the standard of work you expect and the type of help they should provide. If you do not want them to 'give the answer', instead show them how they could encourage children to work things out.

Some of the activities in this book give the accompanying adults a special role within the group, such as secretary to write down ideas thrown up by the children, and you could ask them how much they would like to do in this way for all visits. You should certainly explain in advance (rather than put them on the spot at the museum) that children absolutely love adults to attempt the same activities they are asked to do. Watching adults work and then comparing drawings or answers seems to give children real impetus for their own efforts. They also prefer adults to join in rather than watch them in role-play or dance activities. Some adults are initially shy of joining in or inhibited by perceived lack of skills, but, if they are made aware of just how much the children benefit, they may change their minds.

DRAWING IN MUSEUMS

Apart from its aesthetic role, as in drawing for personal pleasure, drawing is an important means of learning about objects. Drawing forces long periods of careful observation and slow contemplation of the objects, it gives time for discoveries and relationships to be made, and understanding to be encouraged.

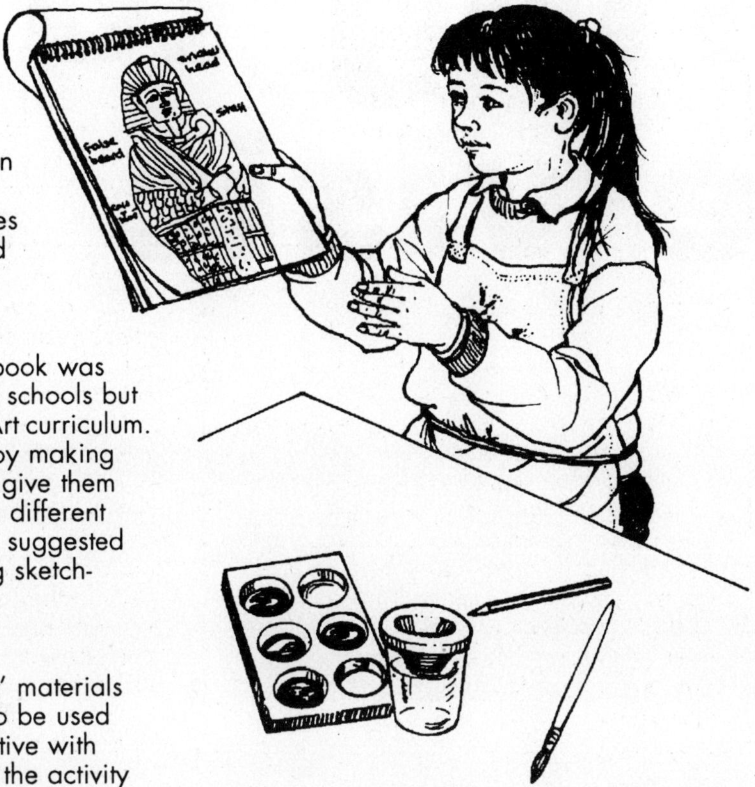

Sketch-books

The practice of keeping a sketch-book was previously only encouraged in art schools but it is now a compulsory part of the Art curriculum. A useful way to help children enjoy making their observational drawings is to give them a personal sketch-book, for use in different areas of the curriculum. We have suggested several ways of making and using sketch-books in the activities.

Drawing materials

Most museums will not allow 'wet' materials such as felt-tipped pens or paint to be used in the galleries. You can be inventive with dry materials, however, and plan the activity so that the painting is done back at school. If children are very careful about dust and collecting up the paper wrappings, oil crayons or pastels can be used for quickly covering large areas of drawings with colour. You will need some moist tissues for the children's hands afterwards.

MUSEUM EDUCATION SERVICES

Most museums believe that one of their main roles is to educate the public about their collections and make arrangements for this. They will have identified someone responsible for liaising with teachers, and many have flourishing museum education departments.

A wide range of activities is covered by the term 'museum education' and each department has its own priorities and specialities. It is impossible to generalise – some museum education departments are quite large while in others there is a single education officer for the museum or even a group of museums. Policies and practice also vary, depending on whether the museum is funded nationally, by the local authority or privately. Some departments provide direct teaching or object-handling sessions, while others offer support and advice for self-teaching such as packs, teachers' notes, worksheets, videos or courses.

In addition, each works on its own range of material such as pictures/art, archaeology, ethnographic collections, open air/architectural sites, natural history/environmental resources and so on. The vast majority of museum education officers have qualifications and experience in the formal teaching sector.

There are no comprehensive directories of museum education services in the UK at present. It is however possible to send or telephone for information about what each can provide. Your local education advisors may have knowledge about and contacts with services available near to you. Once you have located the services that interest you, ask to be put on the mailing lists for future events and projects. These are usually free.

SETTING A MUSEUM PROJECT

If you would like your pupils to contact museums independently as part of a topic they are covering, you can help them achieve success with a little preparation. Stress that museums are about objects and that the information comes from looking at and recording from the objects. You can discuss which are suitable museums for which topics. It will be important to make sure pupils understand how to use a library – much of the information they need might be found more sensibly through encyclopaedias and reference books.

If you are going to suggest to your class that they write to museums for help, discuss what they should ask for. They should avoid the sort of letter that says 'Please send me everything you know about X', because the curator, who may be the world expert on X, cannot reasonably reply and may just send a booklist. Instead, they should concentrate on the things they have been unable to obtain from books, for example, information about what items in the museum are made by a particular person or requesting a list of posters or publications on sale.

Preparing to go on the visit

Planning the visit 1: making a booking

Aim

To give children social confidence and practice in communicating with unfamiliar adults, using the telephone and writing letters to acquire specific information. This activity relates to the English curriculum as well as to the requirements for personal and social education.

Age range

Seven to eleven.

Group size

Small groups and individuals.

What you need

Museum information leaflets, access to a word processor, telephone and photocopier, pens, pencils and paper.

What to do

Once you have decided which museum to visit the children can help make the booking. Depending on your knowledge of the site and the booking system, you can help them to obtain information on the services available, secure a booking form, or make the booking itself. This may need to be done on the telephone, by letter or by filling in a form.

First ask the children to brainstorm the kind of information they need (opening times, booking system, publications and other services available, lunchroom facilities, wheelchair access if required and so on).

If a telephone call is needed, ask the children in groups to plan their conversation and write down their questions so that nothing gets overlooked. Then they could do a role-play exercise to practise the conversation. Suggest that the caller repeats the information received back to the museum to check for accurate understanding and to allow others to record the answers and prompt for missing information. It would be useful if you could enlist the support of the school secretary who could supervise the call and help out.

If it is decided that a letter is needed, ask pupils to write drafts and to read them to the rest of the class. Once they are all happy with the content of their letters they can post them. If a booking form is sent back from the museum photocopy it and ask each child to fill one in.

This is quite an ambitious activity but if your whole school can adopt a policy of encouraging pupils to make bookings they will acquire very useful skills. You could extend the activity to making coach bookings.

Follow-up

After the visit everyone in the class could write a thank you letter on a word processor telling the museum what they enjoyed.

Planning the visit 2: the timetable

Aim

To give pupils experience of planning their work and to make them feel the museum visit is 'theirs'. This activity relates to the Maths curriculum and to the requirements for personal and social education.

Age range

Seven to eleven.

Group size

Small groups.

What you need

Museum plans, pencils and paper.

What to do

Discuss the purpose of the visit and what you all hope to achieve. Go over the work the children will be doing at the site and let them study plans of the building and the written instructions for the activities. Then brainstorm all the things that need to be done, how long will be needed for each activity and what other places, such as the shop and the toilet, might be visited. Decide when and where lunch will be eaten. Discuss also the length of the journey and the time by which you all have to be back at school.

Then ask the groups to draw up their proposed timetables and present them to the rest of the class. Decide together which one will be adopted.

On the day of the visit operate the timetable and once back at school put aside a time to review its success. What errors of judgement were made, if any, and what factors were overlooked? How might the day be planned differently on another occasion? Would one of the other proposed timetables have been a better option to take?

Planning the visit 3: the route

Aim

To practise route-planning and timetable-reading in a real situation. This activity relates to the Geography curriculum.

Age range

Seven to eleven.

Group size

Small groups.

What you need

Pencils and paper. For journeys where you walk or drive (Option A): large scale street and road maps. For journeys where you take public transport (Option B): published timetables and street maps of the route to the museum from the nearest stop.

What to do

Ask pupils to plan the journey to the museum. Just how far you go with this activity will depend on the children's existing map-, index- and timetable-reading skills. Pin the maps and timetables on the classroom wall. Mark the destinations if necessary; some groups will be able to find them for themselves from map references.

Option A: Ask each group to determine the shortest route to the museum using the main roads, and write down features or towns passed along the way. Next ask them whether this is in fact the best route, or whether they could benefit by using different roads to get there faster. Ask the children whether walking would be more pleasant – if the answer is positive, ask them to include on this route a particular feature of interest or a lunch spot. When the route is chosen, ask one group to prepare an itinerary. They should list the towns or points of interest in the order which they will be passed. Another group can make a sketch map, or mark a map you have given them, to show the chosen route.

Option B: Ask each group to work out the route from the timetable, and plan the way to walk from the nearest stop to the museum. Ask different groups to make an itinerary and a map showing the route.

On the day, the children can use the itinerary to look out for the places they will pass. Back at school discuss the success of the plan and how it could be improved on another occasion.

Planning the visit 4: a historical lunch

Aim
To help strengthen the period atmosphere if the visit is connected to the subject of history. This activity supports both the Technology and History curricula.

Age range
All ages.

Group size
Whole class followed by small groups.

What you need
Library books for older children (including historical recipes – see Bibliography), pencils and paper, ingredients or ready-cooked food, baskets, cloths such as clean tea-towels, napkins, or greaseproof or waxed paper.

What to do
Tell the children that they are going to plan a historical packed lunch for the day of the visit. With Key Stage 1 children you should concentrate on the differences between the past and now. At Key Stage 2 you could ask for some research to be done to make the lunch as historically accurate as possible.

Depending on your situation you could enlist the help of your school catering service or there may be parents who would wholeheartedly enjoy entering into this exercise and help with some cooking for the follow-up activity. Remember to allow for any special dietary needs.

Ask the class to help you draw up a list of things to avoid. Your list might include:

- packaged snacks and crisps
- pre-packed sliced bread
- fizzy drinks
- processed cheese
- chocolate bars
- clingfilm, plastic, tinfoil, metal cans.

Now ask pupils to work in groups to plan a cold packed lunch that excludes these items (they may need a little prompting). Groups should present their ideas to the rest of

the class who should be asked to look for anachronisms.
Some possibilities for the lunch are:

- native fruit (apples, pears, plums)
- vegetables (celery, carrots, cold boiled potatoes, lettuce, cress)
- boiled eggs, scotch eggs
- cooked meat or chicken
- cheese
- meat pies, sausage rolls
- Asian snack food such as samosas
- home-made bread, cake and biscuits
- jam, honey, butter
- cold tea, home-made still lemonade, water, milk
- baskets, clean cloths or greaseproof or waxed paper, in which to wrap food.

Follow-up

Enthusiastic classes could try cooking historical recipes. Research the possibilities, decide on the menu and cook or assemble it as necessary to take on the day.

Practising the skills

Using artefacts 1: a simple handling session

Aim

To give young children some experience of working with objects and of sorting them into categories. Classification of objects is basic to the Science and History curricula.

Age range

Five to seven.

Group size

Small groups.

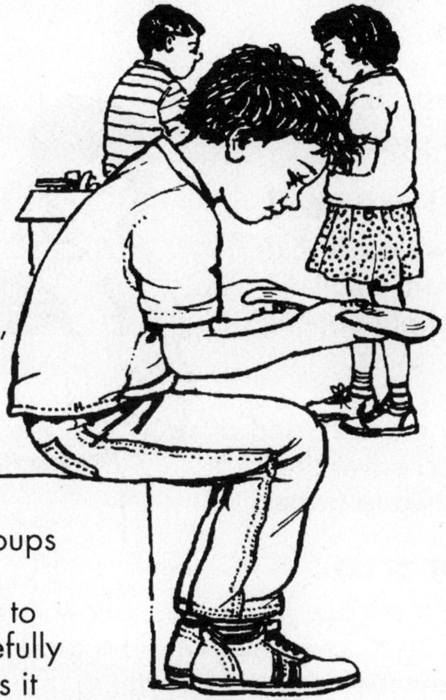

What you need

A collection of ordinary objects from your home, such as a shoehorn, a rolling pin, a comb, – one per child.

What to do

Divide the class into groups and give each child an object. Ask the children to look at their object carefully and describe it. What is it made from? Are there any signs of wear?

Next ask the groups to sort their objects into two piles, one of things that are decorated and the other, plain. The possible categories you can give here are endless: whole/ broken, rough/ smooth, for decoration/utility (not tool/tool) are some examples. Let the children swap objects with the other groups and go through the exercise again.

Using artefacts 2: more than one way to beat an egg

Aim

To help children recognise that there are many solutions to one design problem. This activity relates to the Technology curriculum.

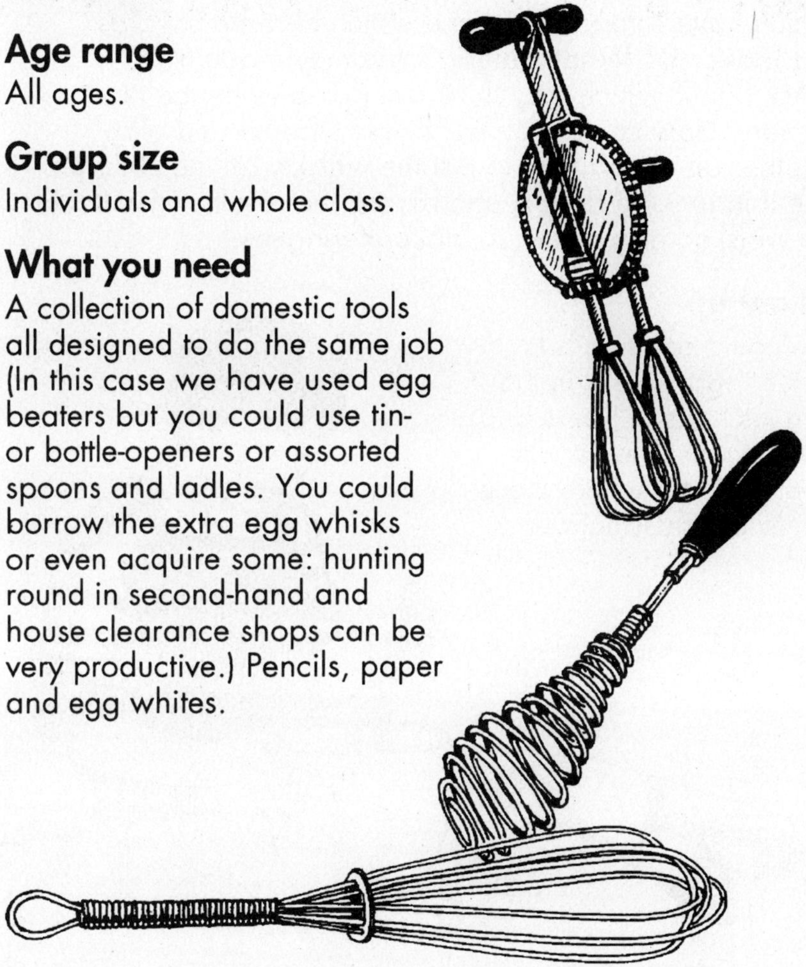

Age range

All ages.

Group size

Individuals and whole class.

What you need

A collection of domestic tools all designed to do the same job (In this case we have used egg beaters but you could use tin- or bottle-openers or assorted spoons and ladles. You could borrow the extra egg whisks or even acquire some: hunting round in second-hand and house clearance shops can be very productive.) Pencils, paper and egg whites.

What to do

Explain to the class that tools which do the same job are often designed differently. Then go on to discuss why you might want to beat an egg.

Next talk about how people in the past have tackled beating eggs. Ask pupils to look carefully at the collection of egg whisks, draw them and describe them. Then they can start to classify the objects, for example: which ones are hand-driven and which by some other form of power? Which have rotary action and which beat backwards and forwards? What materials are they made from?

Ask pupils which they think are going to be the most efficient. How could they test them? Discuss and plan together an experiment to test the whisks. Let the children take it in turns to do this and record the results. (You could use whisked egg whites to make meringues.)

Follow-up

You could ask pupils to look at egg whisks in their own kitchens at home and sketch them. They could then work out where these fit into the classification.

Looking games

Aim

To provide children with further practice in observing the different features of objects and sorting them into categories. This activity relates to the Science and History curricula.

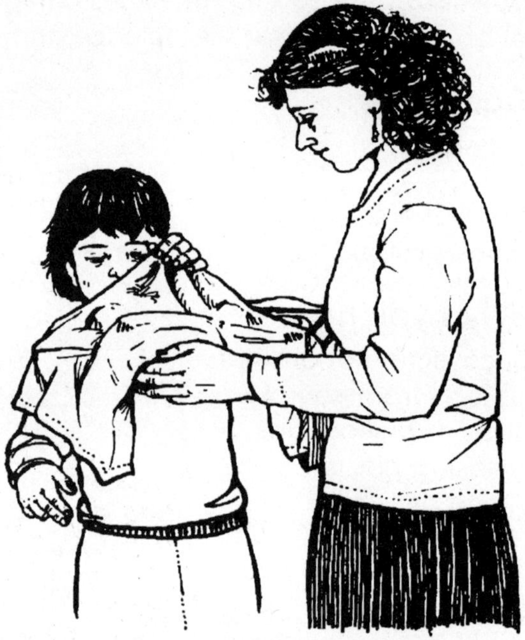

Age range

All ages.

Group size

Small groups.

What you need

Six (twelve for older children) small household objects on a tray, such as an egg cup, a shaving brush, and a cloth to cover them, pencils and paper.

What to do

Show the class the objects, allow three minutes to look at them, then cover them up. The groups then have to attempt to remember and list everything that was on the tray.

Give them another minute to look and then cover the tray again. Now instead of trying to list all the objects give each group a different classification such as rough, shiny, leather, sharp or decorative. They have to list all the things on the tray that fall into that category. Repeat as many times as you wish with different classifications. You could also keep scores to see which group is the most observant.

Describing games

Aim

To help children describe objects carefully using appropriate and/or specialist vocabulary and to show them the vast amount that can be said about the most mundane object. This activity relates to the English and History curricula.

Age range

Seven to eleven.

Group size

Pairs.

What you need

For every child, one household object in a bag so that it can be kept hidden, paper and pencils.

What to do

Sit the children back to back in pairs. Give each child an object which they should then place in the bag so their partner cannot see it. Tell them to write a description of their object without naming it or saying what it is for. They swap their descriptions and without seeing the objects they draw their partner's object from the description alone. They then swap drawings and judge their accuracy.

If you would like your pupils to practise redrafting their work get them to show each other their drawings but still keep their object a secret. Each child now adds to their description to help their partner draw it more accurately.

Looking with fresh eyes

Aim

To help children develop the skills of looking at and thinking about what they see. Role-playing can be done at different levels of sophistication and suits a wide age and ability range. This activity supports all curriculum areas.

Age range

All ages.

Group size

Individuals.

What you need

Any school location such as the dining hall, playground or classroom depending on your 'situation' (see below), clipboards, pencils and paper.

What to do

A very good way of getting pupils to concentrate on a particular topic in a museum is to ask them to think about it from a new point of view. You can do this by asking them to play a role. This does not imply dressing up or acting; it is to do with taking on another person's attitudes and ways of thinking. Here are some examples:

1. You are visiting a historic house and the task is to make sense of what the rooms were for and so how they are arranged in relation to each other. You could ask pupils to take on the role of a maid/footman in this house with a job to do, such as make up the fires, serve food and so on. At the house they have to examine the rooms and work out the routes they would have to take to deliver water to the bedrooms, lay the fires or serve the meals, thus covering the work that achieves your aim.

2. You are visiting a museum where there are lots of examples of designs from the Arts and Crafts movement (or Indian works of art or flower pictures). Your aim is for pupils to develop their own creative designs along these themes. Tell them that the trading manager of the museum wants to market a new range of products called 'Handmade', 'Exotic' or 'Floral' and ask them to make some sketches of designs in the museum that might be used as a basis for these ranges to show to the trading manager.

There is plenty of room for your own creativity in setting up the situations. The first one above could be written out in copperplate handwriting as though it were instructions from the butler to lesser servants. The second could be typed on 'museum' writing paper as an order to the designer.

Here are some dos and don'ts:

- When choosing the roles for the children, start from the aim of the activity rather than thinking of a role and then fitting a purpose to it.
- Prepare carefully to check that the task is possible on the site you choose.
- Roles are very enticing. Do not let the role become so complicated that it takes over from the task in hand. You are not trying to create a fully-formed character as in a play, but to create a challenge which some straightforward research can overcome. Remember that the adoption of a role is a means of getting pupils to look at something from a particular point of view, not to develop a drama.

In school, before your visit, you may want to spend time building the knowledge base that will help pupils visualise the role. For instance, for the first example given above you may want to discuss the differences in life between now and the period of the house. You could get the children to write letters of application for the job spelling out their skills and previous experience.

Here are some suggestions for practising the use of roles by focusing on the school environment:

Objective:	Role:
You want children to be aware of safety issues in the playground and relating to games equipment.	Safety officer who must present a report to local government on whether any special rules for district schools need to be made.

Objective:	Role:
You want children to think about keeping the school clean and tidy.	Adviser to the head, who is about to employ a new cleaner and must draw up a list of what their work will involve.

Making a sketch-book 1: a sewn book made from a variety of paper

Aim

To provide children with their own handmade sketch-book to use and motivate them on a museum visit. The different papers are intended to encourage a creative and experimental approach to drawing because the effect of the art materials varies depending on the paper they are used on. This activity relates to the Art curriculum.

Age range

All ages.

Group size

Whole class and individuals.

What you need

A sheet of thin card for each child, four or five sheets of paper in different colours, textures and weights (these should all be A4 – include cartridge paper, sugar paper, pastel paper, photocopying paper, day glo, or whatever is available), needles and thread, pencils, coloured pencils, wax crayons, charcoal, pastels and clipboards.

What to do

Younger children will need supervision with this activity. Ask each child to select a piece of card and four varied sheets of paper. Tell them to stack the sheets of paper with the card on the bottom, then to fold them in half to make an A5 booklet with the card acting as a cover. Ask the children to make sure the fold is well placed and well creased.

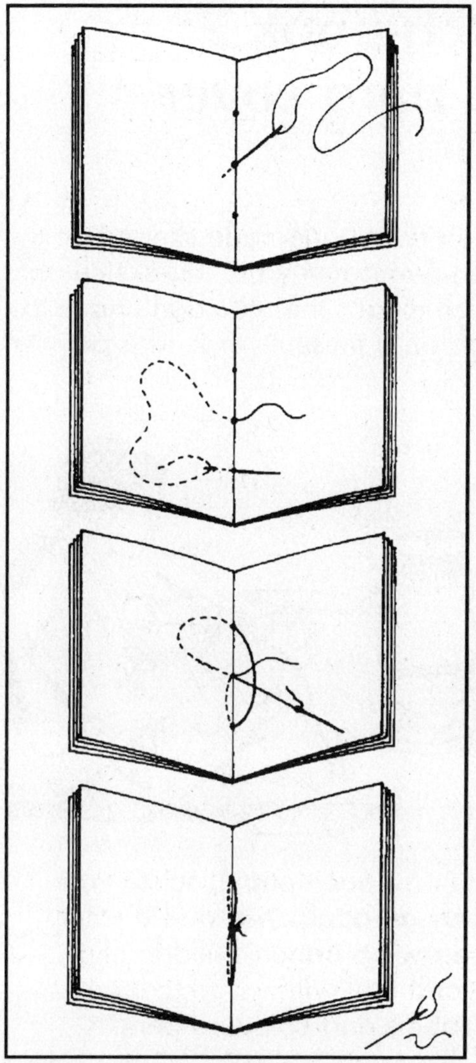

Next instruct them to do the following:

Open out the sheets again and with the needle make three holes in the card and paper along the central fold. Cut a piece of thread about 30cm long and thread the needle. Starting from inside the fold push the needle through the middle hole. Leave a tail of thread about 10cm long inside. Make a stitch along the outside of the fold and thread the needle back through one of the end holes to the inside. Then make a very long stitch inside the central fold to the hole at the other end. Push the needle through to the outside again and then push it back through the middle hole. Tie a knot using the tail that you left and the thread on the needle then tie another knot over the long stitch. Trim off the ends leaving about a centimetre of thread. This is the way that bookbinders gather pages.

In the museum ask pupils to do several drawings using contrasting papers and experimenting with the different art materials.

Making a sketch-book 2: a book with a hard cover

Aim

To provide children with their own handmade sketch-book to use and motivate them on a museum visit. This sketch-book has a hard cover which means that you don't have to equip pupils with clipboards on a museum visit. This activity supports the Art curriculum.

Age range

Seven to eleven.

Group size

Whole class and individuals.

What you need

Heavy card that does not bend, cut into squares or rectangles of the size you want the sketch-books to be (a pair for each pupil), scissors or a Stanley knife (to be used by an adult only) and a safety metal edge to cut against, drawing paper, bulldog clips, a hole punch or a hammer and nail with wood to lean on, ribbon or braid, sticky labels and coloured pencils.

What to do

Give each child two pieces of card. Ask them to draw a line across the end of one piece about 2cm from the edge. Cut through the card across this line. Now, using sticky tape, join the cut bits together again, leaving about a 2mm gap. This will form the hinge of the cover.

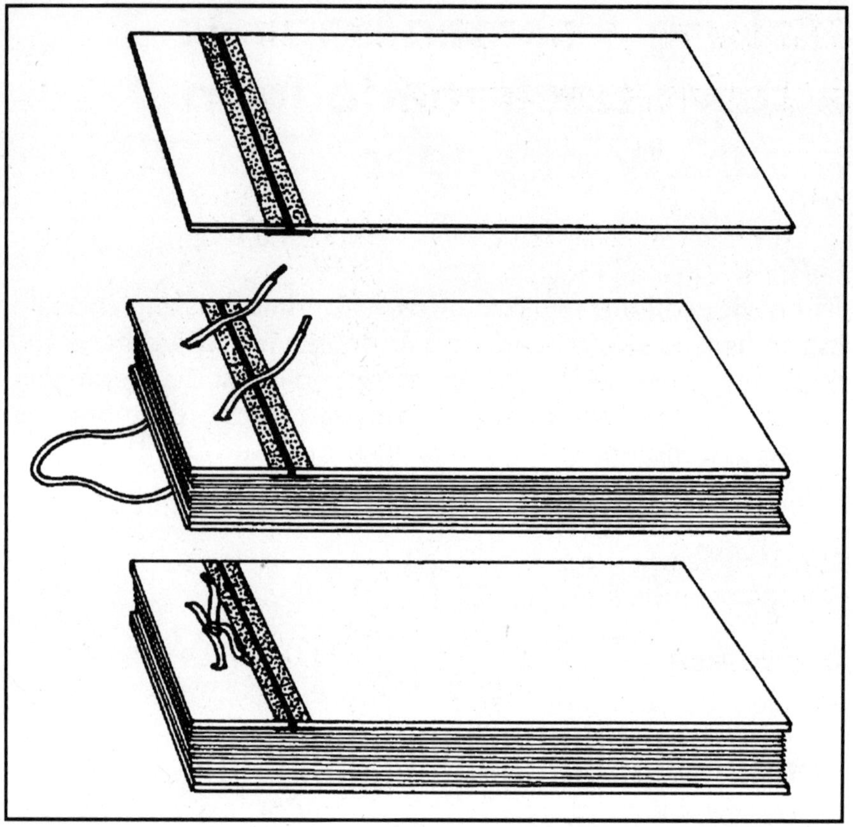

Children should then take some paper for the pages and trim it to the same size as the covers. Put the card and paper in a pile with the cards on the outside. Using a bulldog clip, fix the pile together and make two holes in the hinged end. Use a hole punch or hammer a nail through. Thread ribbon or braid through the holes to fix the pages together and tie a bow or a decorative knot. Put a label on the cover for the owner's name or the subject of the book and decorate it.

A variation might be to cut the book long and thin for drawings of long thin things or small and square for small square things, depending on the subject of your study.

Making a sketch-book 3: a Japanese book

Aim

To produce a notebook in Japanese style which can also act as a sketch-book and to help motivate the children to draw and record. The children could use the book to record their haiku poems on a museum visit (see page 95). This activity relates to the Art curriculum.

Age range

Seven to eleven.

Group size

Whole class.

What you need

A4 white paper, A4 coloured sugar paper, bulldog clips, hammer, nail, thick thread and needles.

What to do

Explain that you are going to use a traditional Japanese method of making a book. Give each pupil four sheets of white paper and two of coloured. The sheets should be folded individually in half to A5 size. Encourage children to press the fold firmly to make the sheets flat, then pile up the folded sheets with the white sheets sandwiched between the coloured ones, which become the cover.

Make sure that the folded edges are all on the same side of the pile. Take two bulldog clips and use them to grip the short sides of the pile to keep the sheets in place. Draw a line on the long side a centimetre away from the cut edges. This will be the spine. Lay the pile on a piece of board or other appropriate surface and punch an even number of holes about two centimetres apart down the line. Thread the needle and stitch though the pile as shown in the diagram. Tie the ends off.

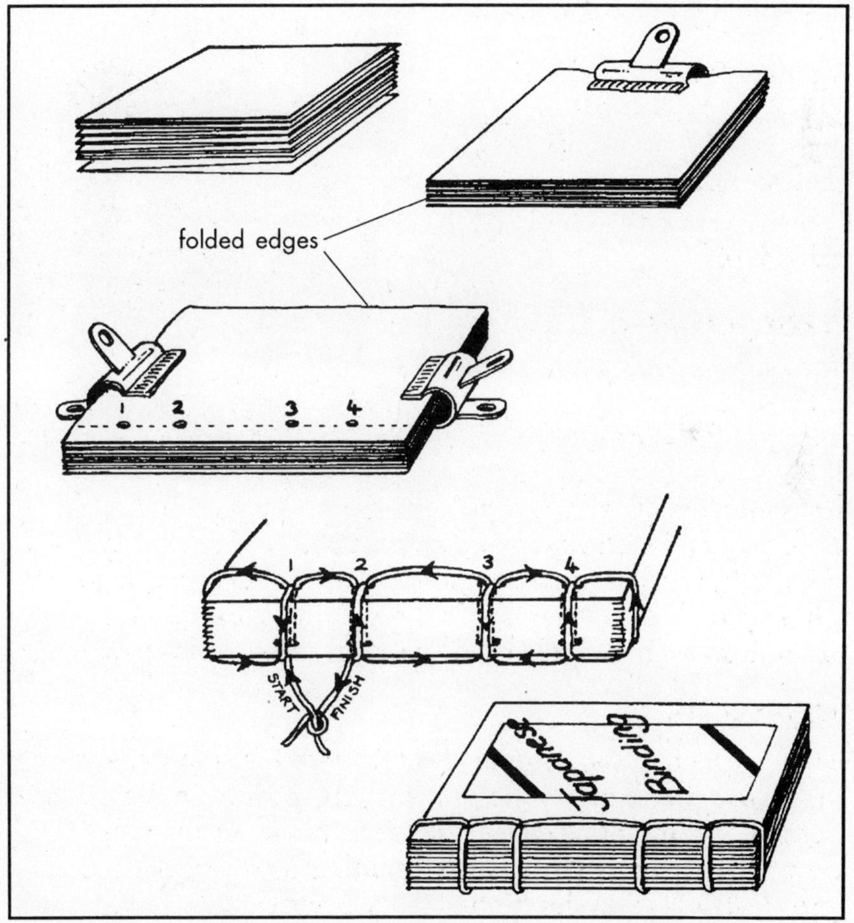

Recording in museums

Drawing 1: series

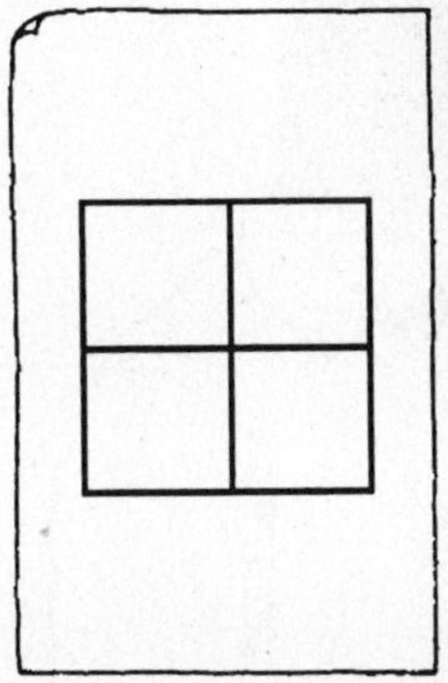

Aim

To develop a way of recording similar items in a museum and to get over the problem of children rejecting their own work. This activity relates to the Art and Technology curricula.

Age range

All ages.

Group size

Individuals.

What you need

Any museum, photocopied sheets with a grid of four, six or eight boxes drawn on them (see illustration), clipboards and pencils.

What to do

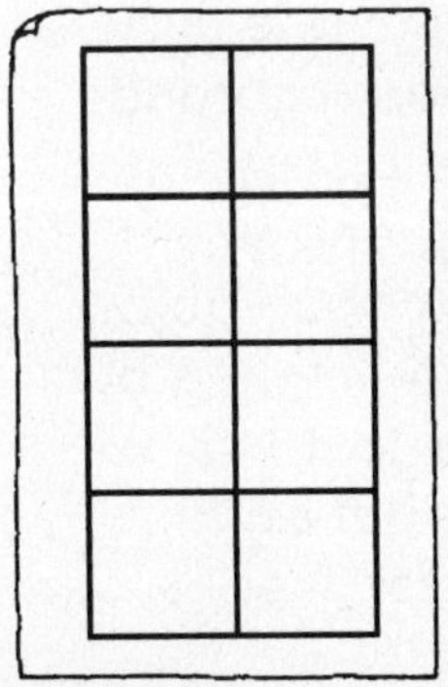

Use this method when you want children to make a series of drawings, for example, of different pattern motifs or shapes. At the museum give out the grids with the appropriate number of boxes. Tell the children that they are to record one design in each box. If they make an error in one box they can go on to the next. By the time they have finished they will probably have forgotten the one that went wrong. The sheets will look exciting and interesting once they are completed and they encourage children to think well of their own work.

Drawing 2: in the frame

Aim

To encourage pupils to focus with concentration on individual objects on display. This activity relates to the Art curriculum.

Age range

All ages.

Group size

Individuals.

What you need

Any museum, plain postcards, a scalpel, sketch-books or paper and clipboards, pencils.

What to do

Take a postcard for each pupil and cut out a rectangle from the centre so that when they are asked to draw something they can look at it through the frame and exclude distractions. They should view the object such that it fills the frame and then draw it to fill their page in the same way. You do not have to confine yourself to rectangles. Cut ogee shapes for medieval or Indian objects, circles for round objects or a silhouette of trees round the edge for a forest animal. Although this might seem labour-intensive, once you have the frames you can use them again in future lessons where drawing is needed.

Writing 1: making notes and labelled diagrams

Aim

To help pupils learn to make notes and do labelled diagrams in a museum setting. The activity relates to the English curriculum but is relevant to almost all school activities.

Age range

Seven to eleven.

Group size

Pairs.

What you need

Any museum with a relevant collection, pencils, sketch-books or clipboards and paper.

What to do

Tell the children that they are going to practise making notes and diagrams. At the museum point out a selection of objects related to something being studied at school. Ask each pair to choose an object that particularly interests them and record it. They should do this through notes and diagrams. They may refer to labels for information or write about it more freely. Give the children about 15 minutes to complete this exercise.

Read out one set of notes and show the related diagram to the rest of the class and discuss them. Are the main points about the object down on paper? Have materials and wear been noted? Has purpose been discussed? Is colour recorded or size estimated? Has the label been copied indiscriminately? Have full sentences been used? (These are probably not necessary for this task.) Has lengthy description been used when it would have been easier to do a drawing to make the same point? Can anyone think of other important things that should have been recorded? Ask pupils to have another go and repeat the discussion. Younger pupils will probably need prompting and you should use the object analysis forms, 'Looking at an object', 'Finding out about history from an object' and 'Finding out about design from an object' (see pages 109 to 111).

Children are often expected to make notes but seldom taught to do it and, therefore, this is an exercise well worthwhile repeating.

Writing 2: a historic diary entry

Aim

To help pupils use and synthesise the information they acquired on a visit, rather than simply to write a narrative describing it (the coach journey, packed lunch, etc.) that may exclude the main purpose. This activity relates to the History and English curricula.

Age range

Seven to eleven.

Group size

Individuals.

What you need

A relevant museum collection, pencils, paper and clipboards.

What to do

If your visit is to research a particular period or event then tell your pupils that they will be asked after the visit to write a diary entry as though it were written at that time. Moving into a Roman villa, a visit to the Great Exhibition or the explosion of Popocatapetl could all be treated in this way. Discuss with your pupils the sort of things people might write in their diaries.

At the museum ask pupils to make careful notes on the relevant objects, bearing the eventual writing task in mind. You might want to give them some guidance: who were you, what were you wearing, what did you see, what did you do and how did you feel are suitable questions for them to think and make notes about. You can compile your own list of questions depending on the collections available and the work you are doing at school.

Back at school ask the children to write the diary entry from the notes that they made. Read some out to the class and discuss the most effective features of the entries.

Diagrams 1: using charts

Aim

To develop a quick and effective method of recording in a museum and to help children ensure that relevant material is selected. This activity relates to the English and History curricula.

Age range

All ages.

Group size

Small groups or individuals.

Name of tool	Materials?	Cutting edge?	Handle?	Draw shape	Purpose?

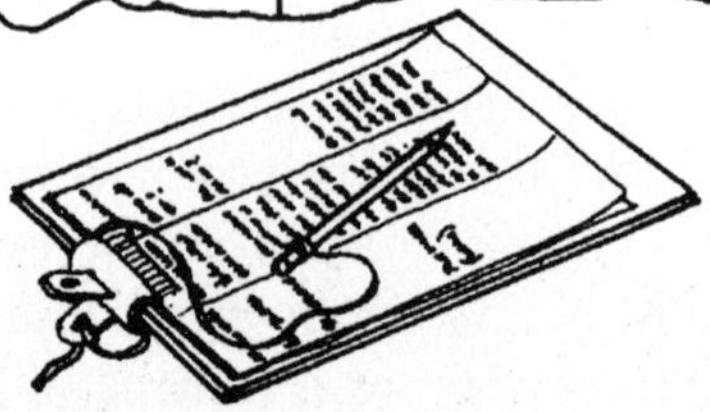

Name of object	What it is made from?	Drawing

Name of object	What I found out	What I still need to know

What you need

A relevant museum collection, a chart copied from page 112 or one of your own (see illustration for ideas), pencils and clipboards.

What to do

In school discuss with the class why you are going to the museum and what you want to find out. Together design a chart on the blackboard that will help to collect that information. (For younger children a simple tick chart might be appropriate.) Other ideas might be as shown in the examples.

Photocopy the chart from page 112, or use your own, and insert the appropriate headings (you or the children could do this); then hand one out to each child at the museum, where they can work individually or in small groups.

Diagrams 2: using Venn diagrams

Aim
To help children classify objects with several variables and to reinforce their understanding of Venn diagrams. This activity relates to the Science, Maths and History curricula.

Age range
Seven to eleven.

Group size
Pairs.

What you need
A collection related to the subject you are studying, some prepared Venn diagrams copied from page 113, pencils and clipboards.

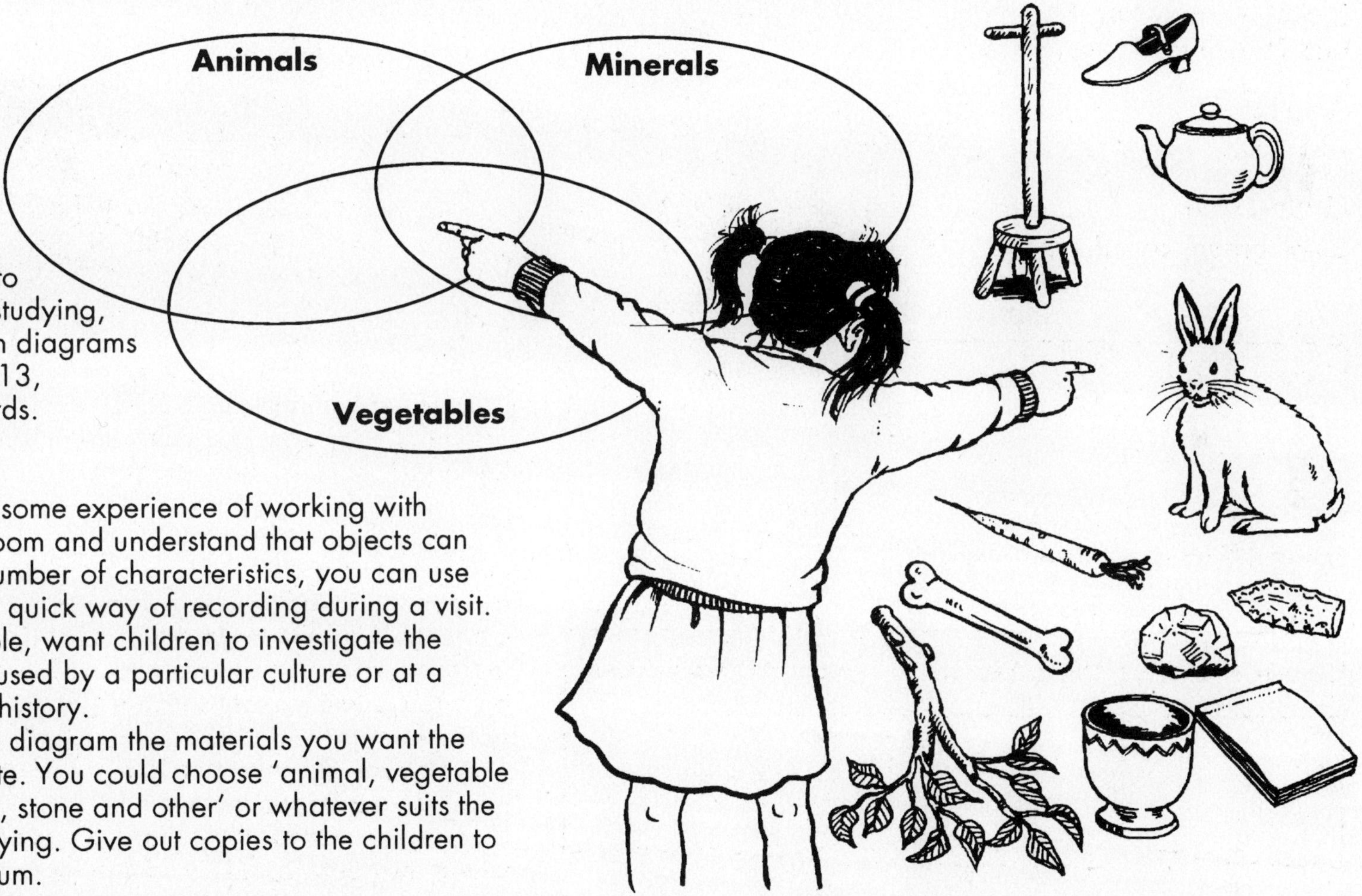

What to do
Once children have some experience of working with objects in the classroom and understand that objects can be classified by a number of characteristics, you can use Venn diagrams as a quick way of recording during a visit. You may, for example, want children to investigate the variety of materials used by a particular culture or at a particular period in history.

Mark on the Venn diagram the materials you want the children to investigate. You could choose 'animal, vegetable and mineral', 'metal, stone and other' or whatever suits the subject you are studying. Give out copies to the children to be used in the museum.

At the museum take the children to the relevant gallery. Ask them in pairs to find objects that fit into the appropriate categories and to write the names of these on the diagram in the relevant places.

Back at school discuss the findings. What were the most common materials or combination of materials? Where did they come from? How do we know? What do they say about the culture being studied?

Archaeology

The wastepaper basket game

Aim

To teach children that archaeologists have to build up a picture of the past from what earlier peoples have left behind. This activity relates to the History curriculum.

Age range

Seven to eleven.

Group size

Whole class and individuals.

What you need

A museum with an appropriate archaeological collection (an archaeological site would be an interesting and useful extra resource), the classroom wastepaper basket and its contents (you may want to doctor these a little to add interest), copies of the activity sheet on page 114, clipboards, pencils and paper.

What to do

Spread some newspaper on a table and then, with much ceremony, tip out the contents of the wastepaper basket. Discuss with the children what someone could tell about the class if they had only seen the contents of the wastepaper basket. Spend quite a lot of time on this exercise and try to tease out as much information as possible.

For older pupils tell them that the contents of the bin are to be buried. Ask them what would survive after a year underground? If someone then dug the rubbish up what would they be able to tell about the class? How would the conclusions be different once some of the evidence had rotted away?

Ask the children to try to imagine what an archaeologist in 1000 years' time would be able to work out about their class from what remained of their classroom. This task can be done at a number of levels. You could debate the cause of the classroom being abandoned (redundancy, a disaster like floods or volcanic eruptions) and the effects that it would have on the archaeological evidence. You could discuss how an archaeologist might work out how many people there were in the class (number of metal chair brackets, numbers in sets of equipment, estimating the number of people who could sit round the available tables). Alternatively, you could simply discuss which materials would survive and which would be destroyed. You should talk about the sorts of things that archaeologists could say for certain, the things that could only be speculated about and the things that archaeologists could not tell from the evidence they have.

When you go to the museum try to get the children to look at the archaeological evidence critically. Give them copies of the sheet on page 114 so that they can record for themselves what they can say for certain, what they can speculate about and what sorts of things they cannot tell from the evidence in front of them. This activity can be done with the archaeological evidence of any period.

Wear and tear

Aim
To help pupils understand that different materials deteriorate over time and that burying objects causes particular damage. This activity relates to the Science curriculum and is relevant to the History curriculum.

Age range
All ages.

Group size
Whole class and small groups.

What you need
A museum with a collection of appropriate archaeological material, clipboards, pencils, paper, a place to bury things and a spade.

What to do
When you visit a museum to study archaeological material spend a little time talking with the children about the damage that those objects have suffered. Ask them to look for signs of wear and tear on the objects.

After the visit divide the class into small groups and tell them that they are going to conduct an experiment to show the effect of burying different materials. Ask the groups to collect different materials they would like to test. Make sure examples of paper, cloth, pottery, bone, iron and plastic are included. Perhaps each group could be allocated a different type of material. Encourage the children to make a record of the items being buried and then bury these in the school garden carefully marking the spot. You could have one burial spot that is dry and another that is kept damp by daily watering.

After five or six weeks ask the children to dig up the items, look to see what has happened, and record the results. Have all the materials deteriorated or have some deteriorated more than others? Is there any difference between the items in the dry ground and those in the damp? What conclusions can they draw from this experiment?

Piecing together the past

Aim

To show children how archaeologists can use pieces of broken pottery to reconstruct the possessions of people who lived in the past and how they can use this evidence to draw conclusions about their lives. This activity relates to the History curriculum.

Age range

Seven to eleven.

Group size

Small groups and pairs.

What you need

A museum with an appropriate archaeological collection, three or four pieces of unwanted patterned second-hand pottery – preferably two sizes of plate, a cup and a jug – a thick plastic bag, a hammer, copies of the circumference measuring sheet on page 115, pencils, clipboards and paper or sketch-books.

What to do

With a bit of drama show the children the pottery and then, one by one, put the pieces in the plastic bag and hit them with a hammer to break them into largish pieces. Give each group a fragment and ask them to work out where on the object their piece came from. When they have decided, ask each group to explain to the rest of the class what clues they found to help them. They might mention the curve, the nature of the rim, any circular indentations or the pattern, for example.

Then ask children to try to draw their object only using the evidence they have in front of them. Groups that have pieces of rim will be able to use the chart on page 115 to work out the diameter and hence circumference of the rim. Display the drawings and compare ones based on the same object. Did some people have more evidence (for example: those with handles, lips or rims) to work on than others?

In the museum ask children to work in pairs. They should find displayed fragments of pottery and discuss together what the whole object looked like, working from the clues they can see and comparing the fragments with whole examples in the museum. They should draw the complete object and label it. This can be repeated with several different fragments.

Back at school you can group the drawings of similarly shaped objects so that the class can make some display posters, for instance 'Roman Samian bowls' or 'Examples of Anglo-Saxon jugs' and so on. Discuss what the pottery tells us about life in the past, for example: there were highly developed skills in the Roman period, the existence of luxury products, suggestion of a wealthy class and so on.

Back garden archaeology

Aim

To help children to get a sense of the history that surrounds them even in apparently unpromising areas. This activity relates to the History curriculum, especially local history.

Age range

All ages.

Group size

Whole class or small groups.

What you need

A museum with archaeology and local history collections, a collection of objects found by your class, clipboards, pencils and paper and copies of the sheet on page 115 and page 114 (optional).

What to do

Ask the children to bring into school things which they have unearthed in their back garden or open ground (not known archaeological sites!). It is likely that you will be able to make a considerable collection even if your school is in a city centre. It may include pottery and bone and is also likely to have bits of building material, old motor bike parts, clear glass marbles from the necks of old pop bottles and possibly clay pipe stems.

Ask the children to sort the collection. They could divide it into different materials, by whether it is decorated or not, or by date based on whether something is older or more recent than something else. (Do not try to give things absolute dates as this is a very difficult activity.) Can pupils think of other ways to classify the material?

Once they are familiar with the finds they should try to identify and record them. Much is likely to be broken pottery, often with blue and white transfer decoration. If you have part of a rim older children might like to calculate the circumference using the chart on page 115.

Go to your local museum and see if the children can identify items similar to the ones they have found. Ask them to look at how things have been labelled and how old they are. If they have failed to identify something in class tell them to ask the curator. Telephone beforehand to say you are coming with your class and a mystery object.

Back at school discuss what these discoveries tell you about the history of your area. You could use copies of the sheet on page 114 'Looking at the archaeological evidence'.

Making a time capsule

Aim

To help children think about the way that objects represent the people who made, used and kept them. This activity relates to the History curriculum.

Age range

All ages.

Group size

Small groups.

What you need

A museum with a display covering the period you are studying, a small cardboard box for each group such as a shoebox, pencils and paper, magazines and catalogues from which to cut out illustrations.

What to do

Visit a museum and ask the children to look at the kinds of items that have survived to tell us about that period. If we could talk to the people from the past today what objects might they choose to represent their lives? Would they be the same objects that survive in the museum today or might they have chosen different ones? Why might the objects have been different? For example, a fur might have been very important to someone in the Old Stone Age but would be unlikely to exist in a museum today.

Back at school the groups should design their own time capsules. Give each group a box. They can put as many descriptions or pictures of things in it as they like such that people in 200 years will know something about them. When they feel they have assembled the contents of their boxes ask the children to choose just ten of the items to represent their group. Each group should present their choice to the rest of the class.

Follow-up

This activity could be extended in a number of ways. You could ask the groups to pass the boxes round to be opened and discussed by each group. Which collection was the most representative, unusual or imaginative? If your school has a building project you might like to assemble the objects and bury them in the foundations. You could ask for objects that represented the locality, the country or the time.

Visiting the past: using a tape recorder

Aim

To give children the chance to record their observations without needing to write extensively. This activity relates to the History curriculum and in this case the study of Ancient Egypt but you could focus on any other culture or period.

Age range

Seven to eleven.

Group size

Small groups.

What you need

A museum with a collection of Ancient Egyptian objects and a small hand-held tape recorder for each group. (If there are not enough tape recorders, this activity could be done in conjunction with another, so that only one tape recorder is needed at a time.)

What to do

This activity works best if you give your class a very tight brief. The activity should give them a very clear reason for examining the museum objects in detail. Make sure that the children know how to use the tape recorder.

Tell the class that they are going to make a radio programme about the building of the pyramids. Ask them to work in groups to plan the programme. They are to conduct the interviews in Egypt (the museum) and the local colour will be provided from descriptions of some of the relevant things that they can see. Conduct a sample interview to show the class what is expected. They could do an interview with the works engineer, a labourer, a tomb painter, an embalmer or someone who had to procure the objects that went in the tomb. They may have pulled off a broadcasting coup by being granted an interview with the pharaoh. They might decide to include a fashion report or to attend a burial. They should plan the programme, including the order of appearance and subjects covered. They will probably need to do some research.

At the museum the children should continue their research in groups. (Are there examples or pictures of the kinds of things worn in Ancient Egypt? What went in the tombs? Can they find out about the life of the Pharaoh?) The interviews should take place in front of the museum cases where useful evidence will be found.

Follow-up

This is an exciting but challenging activity and one that improves with practice. After the visit let the children listen to other groups' tapes and discuss both the weak and the strong points (of the history and the radio production). Let the children repeat the activity in the not too distant future so that they can build on previous experience.

Roman numerals

Aim

To help children decipher written information on objects (both ancient and more modern). This activity relates to the History curriculum.

Age range

Seven to eleven.

Group size

Pairs.

What you need

A museum with displays of Roman material or more modern objects with Roman numerals, clipboards, pencils and paper.

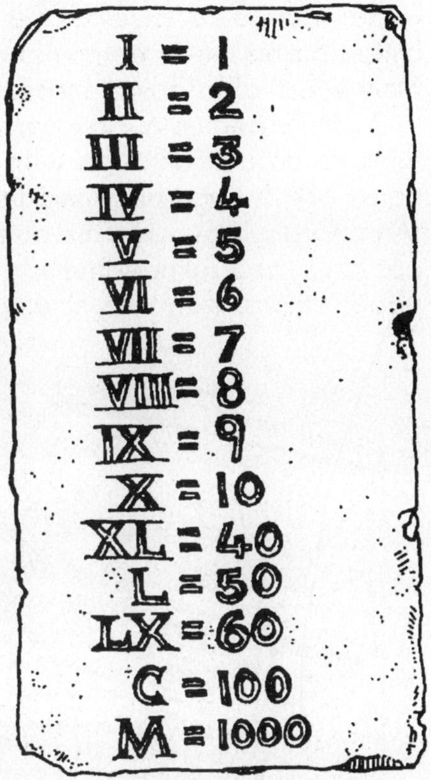

What to do

Teach the children the basic figures in Roman numbers. Then explain that a small unit placed in front of a larger unit is subtracted from that unit and a small unit placed after a larger unit is added to that unit.

Also explain that large numbers are expressed by assembling a number of basic figures which together total the number required so that 1996 could be written as MCMXCVI i.e. M/CM/XC/VI or 1000 + 900 + 90 + 6 and 349 could be written as CCCXLIX i.e. CCC/XL/IX or 300 + 40 + 9.

Note: There are a number of ways large numbers can be written as there are no clear rules as to how to make them up, e.g. 1996 could also be written as MCMIVC. What most often happens is each place is dealt with separately.

This may seem complicated to you, but children enjoy working out the numbers and treat it like deciphering a code.

At the museum set a task that involves working out dates, times and weights from Roman numbers. They may be on Roman artefacts or on later objects such as clock faces, marked on timbers in the course of building construction, foundation stones and memorials. Ask the children to work in pairs.

Follow-up

You could set a quiz where the answers have to be given in Roman numbers.

Roman board game

Aim

To help children think about daily life in Roman history and its impact on individuals. This activity relates to the History curriculum.

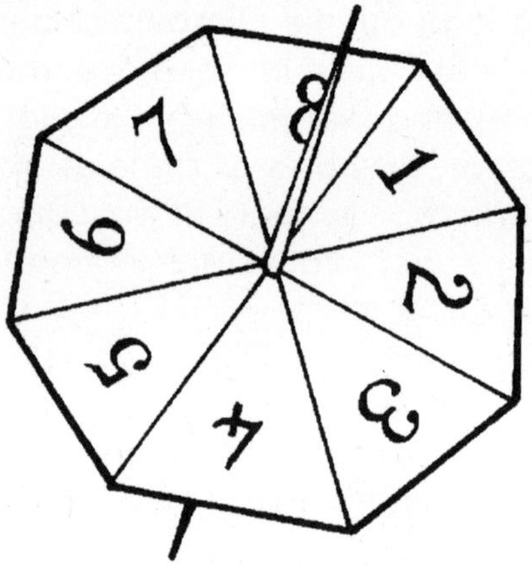

Age range

Seven to eleven.

Group size

Individuals to make parts of the game, and groups of four to play it.

What you need

A museum with a Roman collection, sheets of card to make the game boards, drawing paper, ruler, felt-tipped pen, plain postcards, pencils, coloured pencils, clipboards, a teetotum per game board, counters and glue.

What to do

Start by drawing out some game boards on sheets of card, for your class. They should be marked into squares with a ruler and a felt-tipped pen, like a snakes and ladders board but with six large squares in each row and each square of sufficient size to fit in a child's drawing, say a minimum of 8 x 8cm. Allow 36 squares per board and number them by zig-zagging along the rows (as in snakes and ladders). Number the squares with Roman numerals, starting with I in the bottom left-hand corner of the board.

Cut up some drawing paper into squares of the same size and number them from 1–36 as well. You need enough squares in total for each child in the class both to draw on two or three, plus fill in some extras with the 'up' and 'down' messages (mentioned below). You may need to make more than one game board so that each child can place all their squares.

In the museum, give out the squares of paper to the children and the same number of postcards (excluding two for the 'up' and 'down' message squares). Each child has to find, draw and colour a Roman object for each square and think up a question to go with it, for example, 'What is the name of this huge pot, used for storing wine or oil?' Answer 'Amphora'. They write the question and answer on the postcard, and number it clearly (on the back) to match the paper square with the drawing.

Finally, by thinking about the objects they have seen and from their own knowledge, children have to think of an 'up' message, such as, 'You have been elected senator because of the beautiful new forum you provided' or a 'down' message, such as, 'The wine harvest failed and your business crashed'. They write the 'up' and 'down' messages on separate paper squares.

At school, ask the children to stick down the drawings and 'up' and 'down' messages on the appropriately numbered squares on the game board. Lay the question and answer postcards face down so the numbers show.

To play the game:
Four pupils each have a different coloured counter.
They take it in turns to spin the teetotum and move the appropriate number of squares. They then answer the question on the corresponding postcard. If they answer correctly they can stay there. If they are incorrect they go back to the square they started from (for that go). Landing on an 'up' message means they move five places forward, landing on a 'down ' message means they move five places backward. The first person to reach square XXXVI (36) is the winner.

Mosaics

Aim
To introduce children to a Roman method of decoration. This activity relates to the History and Art curricula.

Age range
All ages.

Group size
Individuals.

What you need
A museum or site with a Roman mosaic on display, pencils, paper and clipboards or sketch-books, large sheets of sugar paper, coloured paper or magazine illustrations cut first into narrow strips then into little squares about one to two centimetres across, postcards of mosaics, scissors and glue.

What to do
At the museum (or site) look at examples of mosaics with the children and discuss how the design was made. Notice the small pieces of marble and stone set in cement. Look at the different colours used and how each individual motif has been made. Do they have outlines? Has shading been used? Are the changes from one colour to another gradual or sharp? Ask the children to sketch some of the designs.

Back at school ask children to design and make their own mosaic. They could copy a Roman original but it might be more interesting to use the Roman technique to produce a new picture either of life in Roman times or of an event today. When the children get stuck encourage them to refer to the postcards for ideas. They should plan out their idea in pencil first on the sugar paper, then start sticking the paper pieces on to this.

Mortaria

Aim

To show children how objects can reveal the needs of the users, and how seemingly simple or 'primitive' items can serve their purpose very well. This activity supports the History and Technology curricula.

Age range

Five to seven.

Group size

Small groups.

What you need

A museum with examples of mortaria (Roman grinding bowls), a modern pestle and mortar (stone or ceramic), gritty inside surface samples of, for example, dried sweetcorn, black peppers, wheat and parsley, (choose items of different size and weight), clipboards and paper or sketch-books, pencils.

What to do

In class discuss with the children the sorts of food that can only be made from crushed grain – bread and pasta, for instance – and the difficulty of producing this before powered machinery was available. Let the children try to crush and pound some ingredients with a modern pestle and mortar. Ask them to tell you what makes the job easier or harder. What is the easiest position to adopt to do the pounding and crushing?

In the museum, look at the Roman mortarium and ask the children in groups to discuss with the accompanying adult what they think the bowl is for. Prompt them to consider the grit pressed into the inner surface of the bowl. Was the grit in the clay in the first place or was it pressed into the wet clay? (The latter, because it is only on the inside.) Why is it there? (To help with the grinding process.) Discuss other significant features (for example: size, weight of the vessel and pouring lip). It is also likely to have the stamp of the maker on the rim. Ask them to do drawings of the bowl labelling the important parts. Ask the adults to assist with the labelling. The children can make another drawing to show how they think someone might stand or sit to use it.

Follow-up

Back at school, the class could experiment to find out how long it takes to crush 25 grams of wheat into flour. Find out how much flour is needed to make a loaf. Ask the children to estimate how long it would take to produce enough flour for one week's bread. Women would do the pounding – what does this tell us about their lives?

If it is possible to pound enough grain, the class could make a loaf and compare it with modern bread.

Painting Ancient Egyptian figures

Aim
To help pupils understand that ancient Egyptians looked as we do, not like their representation in pictures. This activity relates to the History curriculum.

Age range
Seven to eleven.

Group size
Individuals.

What you need
A museum with paintings showing ancient Egyptians, copies of 'How to draw an ancient Egyptian' on page 116, clipboards, pencils, sugar paper (if possible in two shades of brown to match the skin colour of the men and women in the paintings), paints, scissors, glue, a length of paper to make a frieze on the classroom wall.

What to do
Go to the museum and look at the paintings. Ask children to try to pose standing or sitting like the Egyptian figures – they should find that this is extremely uncomfortable, if not impossible.

Explain that people were painted in this way because the artists wanted to show as much of each person as possible, so they painted some parts of the body as if from the front and some as if from the side. This made it easier to identify people and show what they were doing. Ask the children to look at the paintings and, working from the top of the body, tell you which parts were painted facing which way. Ask them also to notice what artists do when several people are standing together, how more important people are painted larger and men generally have darker skin than women.

Give out the photocopied sheets (page 116). Ask pupils to choose and draw from the displays three figures, both seated and standing if possible, in the three empty boxes on the sheet.

Back at school, decide together on a scene from ancient Egyptian life with enough people in it for each child to draw one. Together make a list on the board of all the people present (Pharaoh, wife, slaves, ministers, farmer and so on) and then allocate a person to each child. Give out the sugar paper and painting materials. Ask each child to draw and paint their person, using what they saw and drew in the museum to give them ideas for how to make the actions or role of their person clear. Then they should cut the figure out and stick it on the frieze paper, arranging the figures in such a way as to make the scene.

Follow-up
You could extend this activity on the museum visit by looking at how artists showed, for instance, ancient Greeks, Romans, or saints in early Christian paintings.

Axe heads

Aim

To practise the skills of observation and deduction. This activity relates to the local history study in the History curriculum.

Age range

All ages.

Group size

Individuals.

What you need

A museum with a range of local flint and bronze axe heads, a range of ordinary modern tools used for cutting and hitting (see below), clipboards, drawing paper and pencils.

What to do

In class, look together at a selection of modern tools such as a hammer, a sledgehammer, a mallet, an axe, a saw. As you talk about each, ask the children to suggest what the different head shapes and handles (length and thickness) tell you about how they are used. (For example, an axe has a long sharp edge in order to cut something along a certain line; whereas a sledgehammer has a flat surface which is used to smash something apart in all directions.) Ask children to make drawings of the different examples, labelling them with the clues about their use.

Take the drawings to the museum. Explain to the children that some prehistoric axes took the place of a number of tools. Ask them to study the shapes and surfaces of the ancient axes, comparing them with the different types of tools in their drawings, and see if they can work out how each one was used. Which were held in the hands? Which were fixed to a handle? How do they think this was done? Then they should draw several axe heads, labelling the features which help to show how they were used. Gather together as a group and talk about why it was so important to be able to make tools and fix handles to them, when almost nothing was available in 'shops'. Discuss with the children who they think used the tools. There is no evidence to show whether it was men or women or both who used the axe heads, but can the children make common sense suggestions as to who they think would use particular axe heads according to what they could be used for, their size and so on.

Discuss what these archaeological finds tell you about the local history of your area.

Domestic life

Tableaux

Aim
To help young children on a first visit to a museum to focus on individual objects on display, understand that these objects were used in the past and that there are similarities and differences between life now and life in the past.
This activity relates to the English and History curricula.

Age range
Five to seven.

Group size
Small groups.

What you need
A museum with period rooms or collections of domestic items, camera (optional).

What to do
At the museum allow each group to go separately round the museum with an adult and talk about the things that they see. Tell each group to choose something to tell the other groups about. Once they have chosen they should look at it especially carefully and make sure they discover as much as they can about it. Suitable things might be a dining room, a kitchen display, a collection of dairy equipment, sewing equipment or a collection of toys. Ask the adult to make sure their group discusses what people did in these areas or with these items, and whether there are any similarities with life today. If you have a camera, and the museum regulations allow it, take a photograph of the objects, display or room.

Back at school each group should act out to the rest of the class how their chosen area or item was used. Everyone in the group should mime something they would do in the area or with the objects. The rest of the class have to guess which part of the museum or collection the group concentrated on. Each group should then plan a tableau where they each stand entirely still in their pose. You could photograph each tableau.

A Tudor shadow theatre

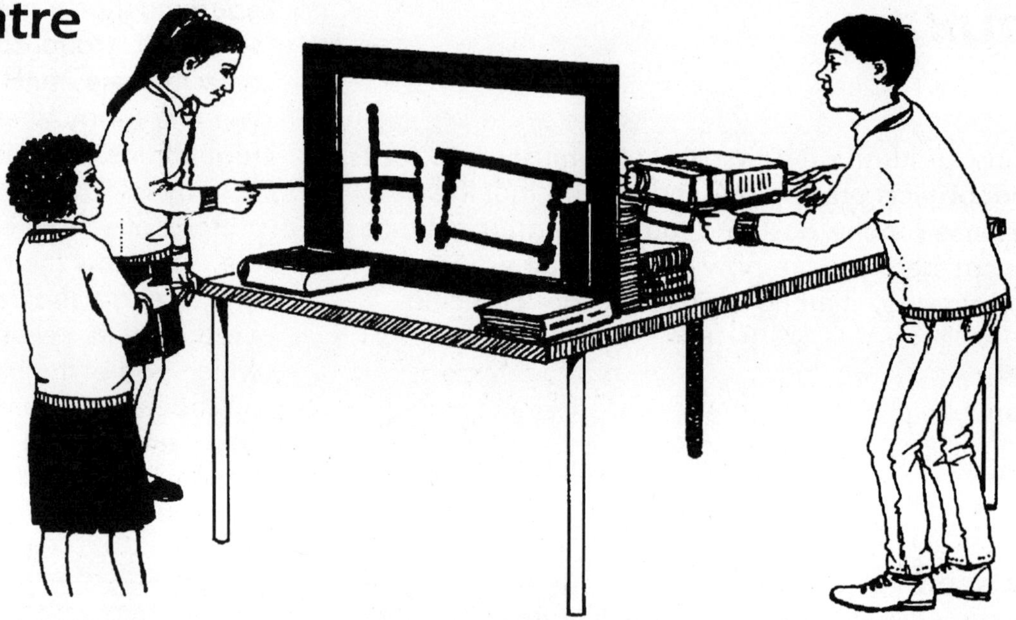

Aim
To help children understand what is meant by a period's 'style' and how this can be seen in the silhouettes of furniture. This activity relates to the History curriculum.

Age range
Seven to eleven.

Group size
Small groups and individuals.

What you need
A museum with a collection of Tudor furniture, pencils, clipboards and paper or sketch-books, black sugar paper, thin green garden canes, sticky tape, card, scissors, a projector, the side of a cardboard box or other sheet of thick card, a large sheet of tracing paper.

What to do
At school discuss the meaning of the word silhouette and let the children practise drawing silhouettes of people and things. Point out that it is the outline that is important and there is no point filling in any detail.

At the museum ask pupils to draw outlines of the kind of furniture that would be found in a kitchen, living room or bedroom of a Tudor house. Then draw some accessories such as jugs or candlesticks in silhouette.

Back at school explain to one group that they are going to make a theatre. Cut a large rectangle out of the piece of heavy card to form a frame. They should then fix the tracing paper across the gap to form a screen. Stand the screen up on a table using books for support. Set up a projector so that the beam shines through the screen from behind.

Other pupils can start to make the furniture. They should use the drawings they made at the museum to draw their silhouettes on to thin card and then cut them out. They need to be a size that fits behind the screen. If your class understands scale you could try to establish a scale but this is not necessary. Each item should be fixed to a stick with sticky tape. Groups can then take it in turn to hold their furniture behind the screen to display Tudor scenes to the rest of the class.

Follow-up
Using reference books pupils could research Tudor clothing and then cut out silhouettes of Tudor people who can be introduced into the scenes. This activity could be developed so that groups plan short plays to enact.

Making hats

Aim

To encourage children to look at the style characteristics of a particular period through making a fantasy hat that reflects the period being studied. This activity relates to the History and Art curricula.

Age range

Seven to eleven.

Group size

Individuals.

What you need

A museum with collections of the period you are studying, 'How to make a hat' activity sheet (see page 117), thin card, scissors, glue, staplers, fabrics and other odds and ends for decorating the hats, pencils, paper and clipboards or sketch-books.

What to do

Please note this is not a costume activity! It is an entertaining way of getting pupils to look at the characteristics of a particular style.

Enlarge and photocopy page 117 on to thin card and hand them out to the children. Explain that these are two ways of making the basic shape of a hat. The first method is to cut a large circle out of thin card, cut a slit from the outside to the centre of the circle and then overlap the card to make a cone-shaped hat. The second, is to make a simple crown (of the head) shape, known as a pillbox hat. Emphasise that these are the basic shapes from which the class can develop their ideas. They could combine the two types of hats, add a smaller pillbox above the full-sized one, or other decorations could be added.

At the museum show pupils the style they are to study. This could be Victorian architecture, Tudor furniture, Indian miniatures or whatever. Ask the children to make sketches of the shapes and motifs used and to record their favourite colours. Back at school these sketches and notes should be used either to add to the hats that they have already made, or to inspire a new appropriate hat.

Follow-up

You could complete the activity with a fashion parade.

Designing a chair

Aim

To help pupils identify features common to furniture design of a specific period. This activity relates to the Technology and History curricula.

Age range

Seven to eleven.

Group size

Individuals.

What you need

A museum display or historic house with items of domestic use from the period you are studying such as clothing, tableware, hangings and furniture, sketch-books, pencils and modelling materials.

What to do

In class tell the children that their task is to design a new chair reflecting the style of the chosen historical period. Divide pupils up so that they design different types of chair, for instance, armchairs, dining chairs, waiting room chairs, wheelchairs and so on.

At the museum, the children should investigate the items on show and look for themes that they think are typical of the period. They can report back what they have found at this stage. Their challenge is to identify details characteristic of that period and incorporate them into a modern setting; they should not replicate an existing design. An example might be a design for a stainless steel chair engraved with Tudor roses. Ask pupils to draw at least three sketches that will help them with their forthcoming design.

Back in school ask the children to make three-dimensional models of the chairs. Set up an exhibition of the results, and ask pupils to award points for a) design (do you like its appearance?) and b) functionality (do you think it does the job for which it was intended?) for each type of chair chosen. Which one wins the most points?

In role: TV set designer

Aim

To introduce pupils to the typical features of a room, for example, a 1930s room. This activity relates to the History curriculum.

Memo

To: Set designer
From: Programme controller

<u>Request to plan a set</u>

We are planning to produce a play on the Great Depression. The action takes place in a small house in the 1930s. Using the collection at the local museum make some sketches of the types of furniture and accessories that you might want to include.

Once you have made a selection write a report for the property-buyer to tell her what to look for.

Age range

Seven to eleven.

Group size

Pairs.

What you need

A museum with a 1930s period room, pencils, paper and clipboards.

What to do

At the museum give each pair a piece of paper with the instructions on the left written on it.

Try not to offer too much help and encourage the children to make their own decisions if they hit a problem. The report writing can be completed at school and examples read out to the rest of the class.

Follow-up

You could move on to writing a report for the costume manager. On this occasion the selection of styles could be based on the study of reference books.

Upstairs, downstairs

Aim

To examine the different types of lifestyle to be found in a big household in the past. This activity relates to the History curriculum.

Age range

Seven to eleven.

Group size

Pairs.

What you need

A museum with period rooms or a Victorian house with 'upstairs' rooms and domestic quarters on display and not too many barriers, a camera, preferably a Polaroid (make sure photography is allowed), books on Victorian social life, pencils, clipboards and paper or sketch-books.

What to do

At school discuss the different people who would live in the kind of rooms you are going to see. Describe the role and life of the master and mistress and of the domestic servants such as the housemaid, the housekeeper and the butler. Give each child a domestic servant's role to research in detail.

At the museum encourage the children to think about the work servants used to have to do for their master and mistress and where they might have done it. If possible the children should sketch a room where 'their' servant relaxed and one where they worked. The children should find something the servant used and something they looked after. Finally, the children should take it in turns to pose in one of 'their' rooms miming an activity they did. They should be careful to take on the demeanour of that person. Pupils could take it in turns to photograph each other in role.

A taste of the past

Aim

To help pupils understand that cooking and eating equipment from the past gives us clues about what food was available at the time. This activity relates to the History and Technology curricula.

Age range

Five to seven.

Group size

Whole class.

What you need

A museum or historic house with displays of items relating to cooking, storing, serving or eating food, clipboard, paper and pencil for the accompanying adult, sheets of card, glue, pencils, coloured pencils and paper. For follow-up activity: historical recipes, cooking ingredients and access to kitchens.

What to do

At the museum discuss with the children the items on display and what they were for or how they were used. From this encourage the children to deduce what ingredients were available to people at the time, or what sorts of foods they were eating and drinking. Make a master list as items are mentioned.

Back at school, ask pupils to make a display of the types of ingredients and food they listed. They could bring in actual samples (and taste appropriate ones), or make drawings and glue them on to a frieze. Pupils can then use the sheets of card to make some menus with appropriate courses and illustrate these with drawings of items they saw on the visit.

Follow-up

You could identify a suitable historic recipe incorporating relevant ingredients and run a cooking and tasting session.

Here is a Roman recipe for stuffed dates:

6 dates per person
shelled almonds or hazel nuts (one per date)
pepper
salt
3 tablespoons of honey

Stone the dates and stuff with nuts and a little pepper. Roll the dates in salt, then heat the honey in a frying pan, fry the dates briskly and serve.

Fill up the dresser

Aim

To provide an appropriate means for children to display their work on domestic items in the past. This activity relates to the History curriculum.

Age range

Seven to eleven.

Group size

Individuals and whole class.

What you need

A museum with a collection from the period you are studying, a picture of a Welsh-dresser laden with objects, brown paper, paint, several metres of cheap ribbon or tape, rulers, pencils, clipboards and paper or sketch-books, card, paints and other art/craft materials as desired by pupils to make their display items, drawing pins and Blu-Tack.

What to do

Make a two-dimensional, full-sized dresser on the classroom wall with brown paper and paint, using ribbon or tape to mark the shelves. Discuss the idea of proudly showing off your best possessions and tell the children their task is to go to the museum and find items to put on the dresser.

In the museum ask the children to sketch up to three examples of items which especially impress them, being careful to record the decoration, colours and so on. It does not matter if several pupils draw the same piece. They should use rulers to help estimate the actual dimensions of each item and note down details of name, materials and date. They should draw the objects as if displayed on the dresser shelves, for example they might want to draw plates as circles standing on edge, not flat.

Back in school, they should make up a picture of their favourite item to place on the dresser shelf. It should be actual size. Although it must be basically flat, materials such as foils, ribbons, tissue paper could be used to achieve an effect which shows the excellence of the piece. You can allow some artistic licence here; pupils do not have to make exact replicas. On the back of each object, pupils should stick a label saying what the item is and any other details they wish to add.

When all the items are ready, display them on the dresser. This must be done as attractively as possible aiming to create a symmetrical balance. Cups or jugs can be hung as if from hooks. Give each child a drawing pin or a piece of Blu-Tack and ask them to place their item. Take time over re-arranging, if necessary, when new items appear, and talk with pupils about balancing or grouping items so that when they have finished, the dresser is attractively arranged.

Model rooms

Aim

To show children how details of domestic life in the past can be worked out through a study of furniture and its arrangement. This activity relates to the History curriculum.

Age range

All ages.

Group size

Small groups of two or three children.

What you need

A historic house or a museum with period rooms. One shoebox per group, paper and clipboards or sketch-books, scissors, coloured pencils or felt-tipped pens, sticky tape, thin card, glue, paint.

What to do

At the museum allocate each group a different room as far as possible. Ask them to sketch each piece of furniture and label it. If there is time, ask them to start to draw some of the accessories such as lamps or pottery. Ask older children to draw a plan of the room, marking on it the location of each piece of furniture and estimates of size.

Once back at school tell the children that they are going to reconstruct their rooms in shoeboxes. Each group should paint the inside of the box to represent the walls and floor. Then they should redraw the furniture on to thin card and draw a tab on the bottom. Having painted the furniture appropriately, they should allow it to dry. Tell the children to cut it out, bend the tab back and glue the furniture into position. Accessories can be added.

Follow-up

Depending on the various sorts of rooms available to study, you could use this activity to contrast the layout of similar rooms at different periods or different rooms within one house. The children could make a period dolls' house for the classroom or create a fantasy world.

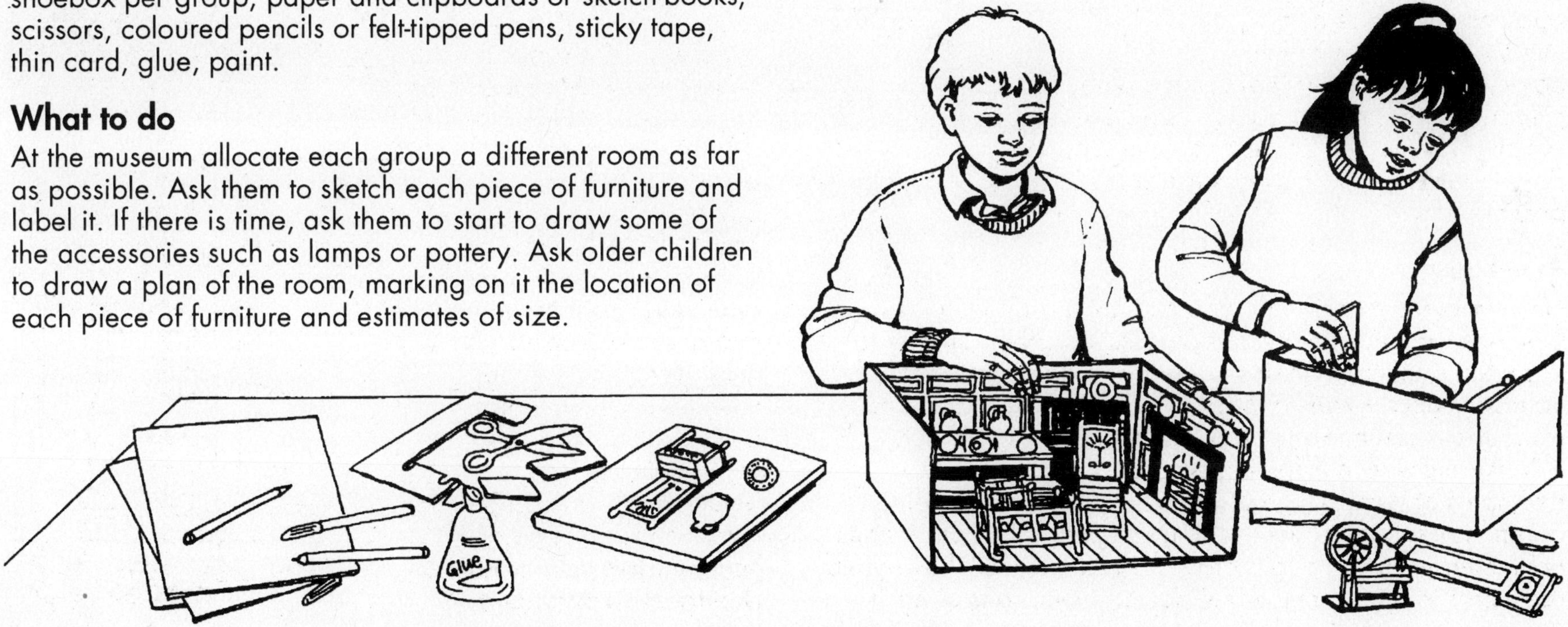

Textiles and dress

In role: a textile designer

Aim
To make children look closely and critically at fabric designs as a preliminary to their own design activity. This activity relates to the Technology curriculum.

Age range
Seven to eleven.

Group size
Individuals.

What you need
A museum with textiles on display, clipboards and paper or sketch-books, pencils and coloured crayons.

What to do
This is a role-playing exercise that asks pupils to look at a broad range of items and then make a selection based on particular criteria.

At the museum give the children the following instructions which could be presented in the form of a design brief:

'You are a textile designer employed by a large furniture store. They have decided to produce a series of fabrics based on the collection at X Museum called 'Orient', 'Arts and Crafts' or 'Stuart' (select as appropriate). Go to the museum and look at the fabrics and objects on display. Select examples of design motifs that you think might be used to inspire a new range of fabrics for the modern home. Record the colour ranges that are used in the originals. Choose three designs that you think might appeal to the art director and do some sketches showing the colours you would use.'

Back at school ask the children to use their sketches to draw pieces of furniture (including curtains and linen as well as sofas and chairs) that they think best suits their particular design. You could ask them to suggest types of fabric that could be used, for example: cotton, linen, vinyl. Once the design proposals are completed, have a discussion about them with the class.

Repeating patterns

Aim

To help pupils understand repeating pattern designs and help them to develop their own. This activity relates to the Maths and Art curricula.

Age range

Seven to eleven.

Group size

Individuals.

What you need

A museum with a textile collection, clipboards, pencils, paper, photocopier, coloured pencils or paints, and (optional) block printing equipment.

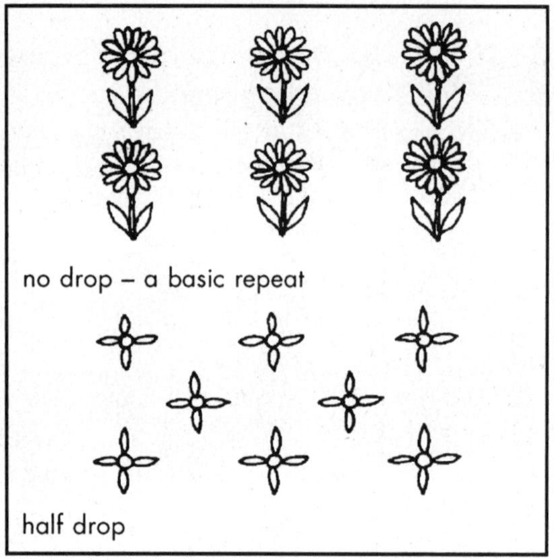

What to do

Discuss with the children how many textile designs are made up from repeating patterns. At the museum, look at a number of examples together and identify the way in which the pattern repeats. In some cases it is just copied across the fabric and down it but in other cases the repeating pattern is more complex. A mirror design may be incorporated or the pattern may be dropped by half a motif.

Ask the children to try to identify the pattern block. This is the complete motif that will then repeat. It is sometimes very difficult to trace the edges of it especially when you are looking at something complex, such as a paisley design, so choose simple repeats to start with. Ask pupils to draw the basic pattern block. Now provide them with a sheet of paper divided into four rectangles. In each rectangle they should draw a different pattern block.

Back at school the children should decide which block they like best. Tell them to cut it out and then you can use the photocopier to develop repeating patterns by making a few copies and then arranging them as series of copies either as a basic repeat or as a half drop. The children can experiment with different colour combinations by colouring in the photocopied patterns. Once they have settled on a pattern they like and that works as a repeat, they could make a block for printing on paper (for gift wrap) or fabric.

Maths from patchwork

Aim

To help pupils see that creative work is often based on very accurate and careful design and execution. This activity relates to the Maths and Technology curricula.

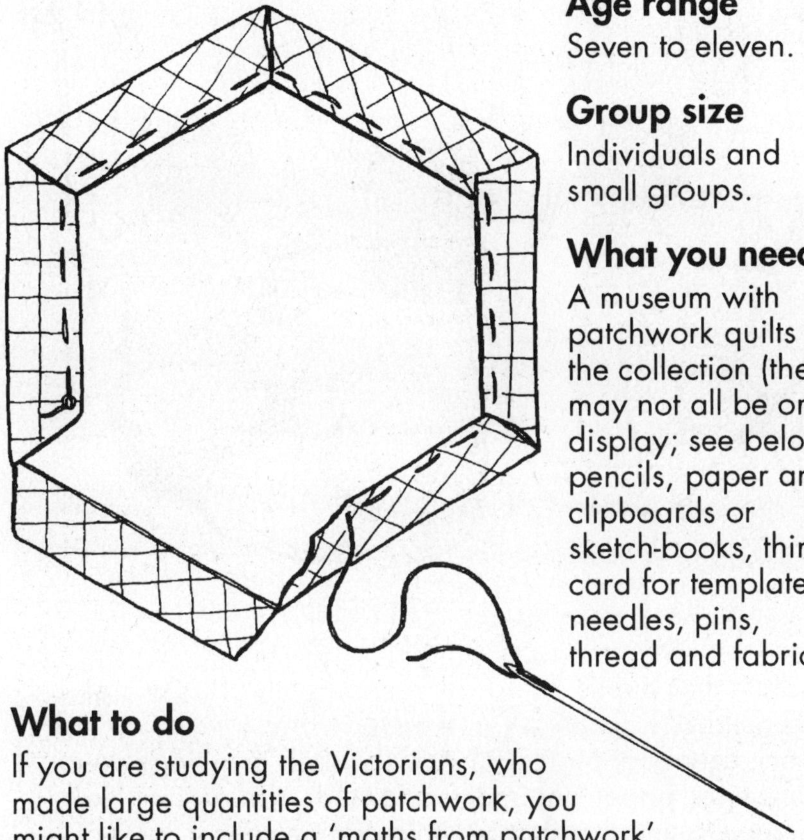

Age range

Seven to eleven.

Group size

Individuals and small groups.

What you need

A museum with patchwork quilts in the collection (they may not all be on display; see below), pencils, paper and clipboards or sketch-books, thin card for templates, needles, pins, thread and fabric.

What to do

If you are studying the Victorians, who made large quantities of patchwork, you might like to include a 'maths from patchwork' project. The children can become familiar with words such as squares, triangles, diamonds, 6- and 8-pointed stars and hexagons during this activity, and they can investigate tessellation and discover which types of shapes fit together.

Visit the museum and look at examples of patchwork. It may be possible for one of the curators to get some examples out from store as many are too large to put on permanent display. Also ask to see smaller quilts for cots or dolls. Look at the overall design of the patchwork and the types of material used. Ask the children to make sketches of the different designs and how the shapes fit together.

Back at school tell the children they are going to make sections of the design. A cot cover is probably as ambitious as any class can usefully get. You may want to divide the class in half to cut out card templates and have one half working on squares and octagons and the other on hexagons and diamonds. Unless your pupils are very accurate in cutting out then you may be better off asking a willing adult to cut out the templates. Inaccuracy at this stage leads to serious problems later.

Next they should tack fabric round the card template shapes. Emphasise the need for accuracy at all stages and check that the fabric is carefully tacked before going on to the next stage.

Get pupils to sew the shapes together and be sure that they are firmly secured at the corners.

Use the sewing enthusiasts in the class to start to sew the motifs together and use any willing adult to help complete the patchwork.

Silhouettes

Aim

To help children understand that the outline of fashionable dress changes over time. This activity relates to the History curriculum.

Age range

Seven to eleven.

Group size

Individuals.

What you need

A museum with a costume collection, sketch-books or clipboards and paper, pencils, cardboard templates of male and female bodies (see pages 118 and 119), black sugar paper, frieze paper, scissors and glue.

What to do

At the museum ask pupils to make a drawing of the outline shape of the clothes every ten years or whatever suits the collection and period that you are studying. (Note: the changes within a period can be very subtle.) Do not let this activity degenerate into a struggle to draw figures accurately. Have prepared a male and a female figure template that pupils can draw round lightly. This will give them a start.

Back at school pupils can transfer their drawings on to black sugar paper and make a 'dated' fashion parade to display. Discuss the changes that can be seen.

Follow-up

These figures could be used in a shadow theatre production like the one on page 44.

Period paper dolls

Aim

To show the details of fashion in the past. This activity relates to the History and Technology curricula.

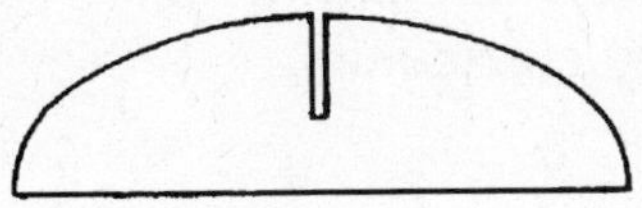

Cut this shape from cardboard and use as a stand to help the doll stay upright.

Age range

Seven to eleven.

Group size

Small groups.

What you need

A museum with a costume collection, clipboards and paper, pencils, coloured pencils, scissors, cardboard, figure templates (see page 118 or 119).

What to do

One way to study fashion is to make period dolls in paper. Give each group a cardboard figure template. This could be a man, or a woman, depending on the collection that is to be looked at and the purpose of the study. Each child should take turns to draw round the template on to some card and cut out their own cardboard figure. Then they can draw round their own template on to sheets of paper.

At the museum the children should use their sheets of paper to record different outfits for the doll, drawing them on to their figure outlines and making sure that the outfits are the correct size to fit over their cardboard figures. They will need to add tabs at shoulders, waist and hips to secure the costume to their cardboard 'dolls' and you may need to intervene to ensure that these work. The bits and pieces of the outfit can be selected from different displays and you may like to suggest that the children look for an outfit for a named occasion such as a visit to the seaside or a dance.

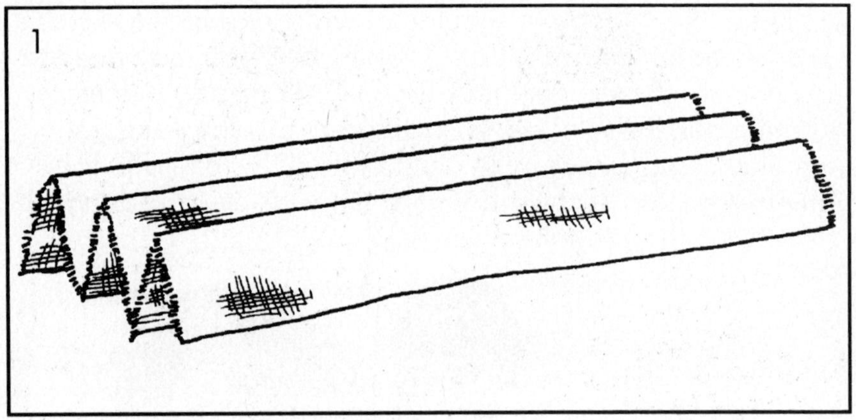

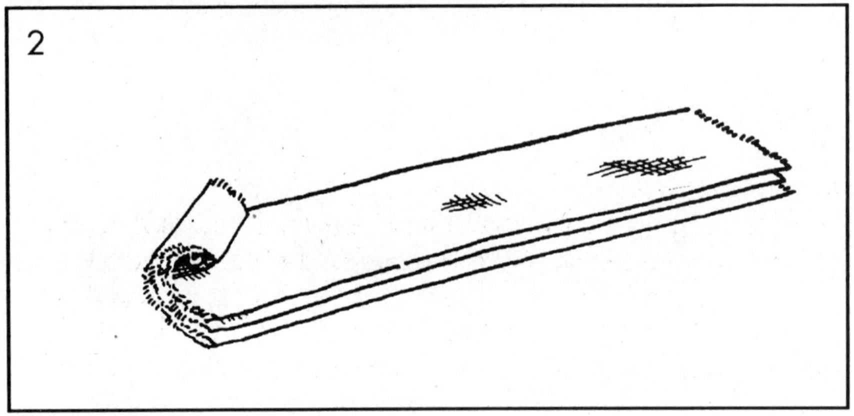

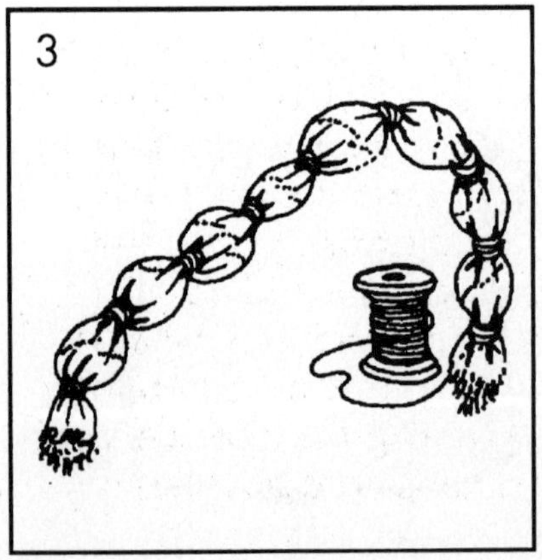

Tie-dye class turban

Aim

To produce a length of tie-dyed turban material in Indian style, using the contributions of the whole class. This is a useful collaborative activity which gives the children the opportunity to explore an important textile technique. This activity relates to the Technology curriculum.

Age range

Seven to eleven.

Group size

Individuals and whole class.

What you need

A museum with examples of tie-dyed fabric, strips of fine cotton 20cm by 50cm for each member of the class, scissors, sewing cotton, two colours of cold water dye (non-toxic), a sewing machine and iron.

What to do

Go to the museum and ask the children to look at examples of tie-dyed cloth, turbans and pictures of people or mannequins wearing turbans. This may be part of a visit to study India or clothes. You could also look for other items of clothing that are not tailored and that rely on wrapping to shape and secure them.

A turban cloth can be up to 30 metres long and dyed. You will find some of the tie-dyed fabric very delicately patterned. Some of it is done with small round dots but for this activity the children will produce patterns that are diagonal or chevron shaped.

Back at school prepare the two cold water dyes and give the children instructions on the care they will have to take to

avoid spillage. Give every child a piece of dry washed cotton cloth about 25cm by 50cm. To make a chevron pattern show pupils how to fold the fabric in half lengthways and then in half again so that they have a long narrow concertina of cloth.

They should then roll the cloth up tightly at an angle (of about 45 degrees) and hold it so that it does not come undone, securing it with rubber bands at each end.

Next ask the children to do the following:

Take some sewing thread and wind tight bands about half an inch or more in width round the fabric. If this has been done well then the places with cotton thread on will be covered too tightly for dye to get through when the cloth is dipped in dye. When they are satisfied with the bands of thread the cloth should be dipped in one of the dye baths. Remove the cloth from the dye after about 60 seconds or when it looks as though the dye has soaked through all the fabric and taken. Wash the roll in clean water to remove excess dye and place on a radiator to dry a little. They can now unwind some of the thread bands and add further ones in different places and then dip the fabric in a second colour, repeating the above. They will get better effects if they start with a light dye and move on to a darker one. Allow the roll to dry a bit and then take all the thread off. Open out the fabric and dry and iron it. NB: Due to the length of time the above part of the activity can take, it may be easier to allow only half of the class at a time to do their dyeing. Once they have all dyed their fabric, the turban can be made on a separate occasion.

To make a turban join all the fabric strips by their short ends so that in a class of 30 pupils you will end up with a narrow strip about 15 metres long – iron again. Invite an Asian parent to show the children how to wind a turban. They may need help folding and pleating the cloth because a careful hand is needed so that it keeps a good shape when being worn.

Tapestry comic strips

Aim
To give children practice in unravelling the meaning of large, complex tapestries. This activity relates to the English curriculum.

Age range
Seven to eleven.

Group size
Individuals.

What you need
A museum or historic house with large tapestries (including lots of people) on display, pencils, paper and clipboards or sketch-books.

What to do
At the museum show the children the tapestry and explain that often several stages of a story are shown in separate areas of the tapestry. It is up to the viewer to decide what is happening and put the episodes in the right order.

Ask the children to make a sketch of the whole tapestry showing all the figures by drawing stick people. Then they should put circles round groups of figures that appear to be talking to each other or engaged in the same activity. Ask the children to try to put the separate groups of people into order and redraw them in the style of a comic. Next, they should imagine what the people in these groups are saying to each other. Ask them to write speech bubbles with the people's comments, and below each group they could write a piece of narrative as seen in comics.

Making a sampler

Aim
To introduce pupils to a range of embroidery stitches and to a historic pastime. The activity relates to the History and Technology curricula.

Age range
Seven to eleven.

Group size
Whole class.

What you need
A museum with a range of samplers, pencils, paper, even-weave fabric, needles and embroidery thread.

What to do
Discuss education in the past and the fact that many girls in the Victorian period were employed as servants, where they were expected to be able to sew neatly when making and mending garments. Sewing, therefore, was an essential part of their upbringing. The girls who were part of the upper classes were also taught to sew. However, this was a pastime similar to playing the piano. They made samplers to show off their skills in embroidery. They also used to sew their initials delicately on to items such as handkerchiefs.

At the museum, look at as many examples of samplers as you can. Look at the colours used and the fineness of the stitching. Ask the children to take note of the sayings included and the names and ages of the people who did this work. Ask them to sketch some of the designs.

Back at school teach the children simple running stitch and cross-stitch and how to count the threads so that each stitch always goes over the same number of threads in the cloth. Ask each child to draw out the design for a small sampler (such as their intials, name or an alphabet, depending on time available) and then to sew it.

Painting, drawing and sculpture

Developing a narrative from a painting

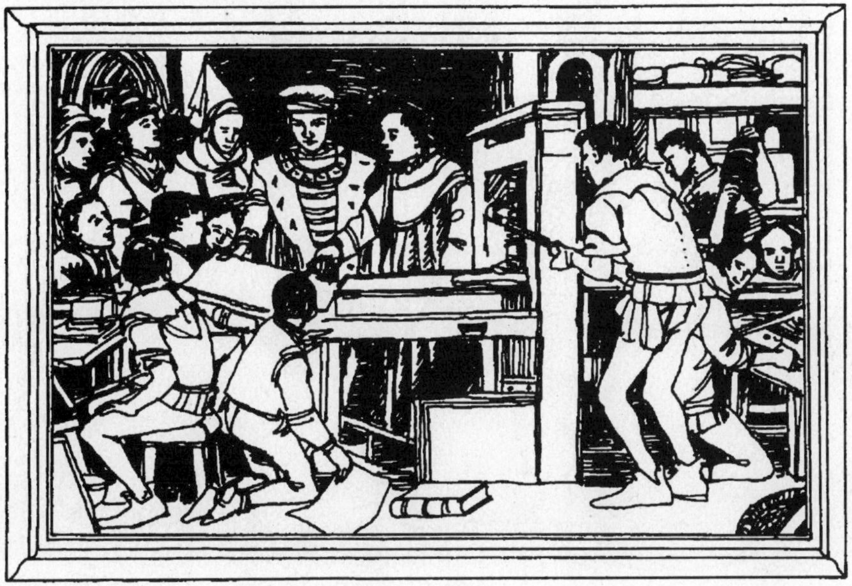

Aim

To help pupils understand how full of noise, incident and comment many paintings are, if they are looked at for long enough. This activity relates to the Art curriculum.

Age range

Seven to eleven.

Group size

Pairs and individuals.

What you need

A museum with a collection of pictures of people doing things (not just posing), clipboards, pencils and paper.

What to do

In the museum allocate each pair to a painting. Ask the children to talk to their partners and make notes on the following: the weather, the time of day, the location, the people in the picture, what seems to be happening at the time, what they think will be likely to happen next. Is there any talking taking place? What sort of things might be being said?

When they have thoroughly explored the content of the painting, allocate each child an individual figure in the painting. Ask them to write a description of what is happening in the painting from that person's point of view (so introducing the element of characterisation in what they produce). They can base it on one of the following formats: a diary entry written later on; an interview given to a policeman or to a media interviewer; an on-the-spot reporter caught up in the action.

When they have finished, sit the children in turn in front of their picture. Ask them to read out their narrative. Can the rest of the class work out which figure is speaking?

A dialogue between two portraits

Aim
To help pupils use flights of fancy as a way of encouraging them to notice the clues to personality in a portrait. This is not a History activity as they are not trying to identify real facts about an actual person. This activity relates to the Art and English curricula.

Age range
Seven to eleven.

Group size
Small groups.

What you need
A museum or historic house with two large portraits displayed fairly close together (completely unknown people are generally better than famous ones) and a hand-held tape recorder for each group if possible.

What to do
Sit each group in front of one portrait and ask them to look at it for clues to that person's nature. Make up a suitable name for them. What are they thinking about? What have they just said? What would be their favourite food? What makes this person happy? What upsets this person? What does this person want as a birthday present? Be as random as you like with your questions.

Once pupils have started to build this character move to the other portrait and ask them to answer the same questions. Then ask them: in what ways is this person similar to the last person? In what ways different? Imagine that one met the other – how would the conversation go? Ask pupils to make a recording of the conversation.

Groups working on other portraits could join the others and discuss their characters. The two groups could develop a dialogue.

Follow-up
Having looked at the details of portraits in this way, pupils could go on to do their own creative work, either through painting their own self-portraits or developing characters in stories.

Looking through closed eyes

Aim

To help pupils understand composition. The activity shows them how to identify which are the most significant features of a painting or item and how these can be used to start off and 'anchor' a drawing or painting. This activity relates to the Art curriculum.

Age range

Seven to eleven.

Group size

Individuals.

What you need

A museum or gallery with large-scale paintings, clipboards, paper, soft drawing pencils.

What to do

Arrange the children in front of a large painting or object so that they can see all of it: they will need to stand well back. Ask them to close their eyes for all but a crack, and to look at the painting. Give this plenty of time. The aim is to see how, when they do this, all the tiny details drop out of the image, leaving only a few strong main lines, bold shapes, areas of bright colour or bright light which are the backbone of the picture (in abstract paintings, this can help you find areas and shapes which dominate in the picture while other areas recede, and a three-dimensional effect is created). Discuss with the children which are the strong features in the picture you are facing. Repeat this with two or three more paintings.

At the last one, give out the drawing materials and ask pupils to mark out the painting starting by putting in the most prominent features first. Discuss and compare the results. Then they can select their own painting or object and repeat the exercise as many times as required. As the last exercise, ask the children to fill in the supporting detail as well.

Back at school, the pupils can make some finished paintings in the above way, of objects or scenes they can find around them (rather than painting from memory or the imagination).

Make your own art slide show

Aim

To help children understand abstract art and see how the way colour is applied plays such a major part in the appearance of any artwork. This activity relates to the Art curriculum.

Age range

All ages.

Group size

Individuals in class,
groups of six on the visit.

What you need

A museum display of abstract paintings, plastic transparency slide frames, sheets of overhead projector film cut into slide-transparency sized pieces, felt-tipped pens, a slide projector focused to produce as large an image as you can manage and a room or area that can be blacked out.

What to do

Give out the pens and pieces of film, and let pupils draw or colour on to them. They can do a miniature scene or figure, or work in spots or patterns of colour. Then they make up the slide, mark the bottom right corner, and project it. Next you want to allow time for experimentation. This activity lets pupils create massive colourful works and unusual effects. There will probably be wonderment at the results, as tiny details take on great prominence, and the colours are transformed by the light passing through. If you have marked the bottom right corner of the slide, you can see what effect it has to re-project the slide in different orientations until the most pleasing is found. Two or more pieces of film can be put into one slide-mount and projected together. Pupils might want to make a sequence of slides and give a small presentation.

On the visit to the gallery, give the groups of pupils time to look at a range of abstract pictures. Then ask each group to nominate its favourite, and for one member of the group to make a small presentation to the rest of the class about why they chose that image and what their reactions were.

Keeping the pencil on the paper

Aim

To help pupils understand how some artists or sculptors want to capture the *idea* of an object, place or person, rather than faithfully show all the exact real-life details. This activity relates to the Art curriculum.

Age range

Seven to eleven.

Group size

Individuals.

What you need

A museum with abstract paintings or objects, large sheets of paper, drawing boards and an interesting range of different drawing materials such as biros, heavy and light pencils, wax crayons (charcoal is best avoided in the museum).

What to do

In the museum give out the drawing materials; it does not matter who has what or if everyone has the same.

Start by telling children to place the tip of the pen or pencil anywhere on the paper. Now they must look up and move the pen or pencil around their paper without looking at the paper again or lifting the tip. They should draw the room they are in, concentrating on the straight lines they can see. They must look at the room very carefully as they do this and there is no need to rush. Tell them that if the pen drops off the edge, just put it back on again and continue. They can turn around if they want. Tell them not to look at their drawing until you say they can.

When you think they are ready, look at the drawings together. Look for the 'idea' of the room in the straight lines. Ask children to tell you what things have been captured, and which have not been recorded.

Now tell the children to change drawing materials and use a fresh piece of paper. They should repeat the exercise again, this time with eyes closed, and draw an object they have just seen in the room. With their eyes open, they can draw the object again, thinking about a particular mood or feeling such as joy, being too hot, fear or mischief.

Now ask pupils to go and look at the abstract paintings/objects, looking particularly at the lines and shapes used and discussing how these might represent the feeling the artist had while he or she was painting the picture or making the object. Discuss how curved edges might suggest feelings of peace while zigzags could represent chaos or disquiet. (Wassily Kandinsky's *White Zigzags* suggests disorder. This is in contrast to many other abstract artists who use formal shapes, such as triangles and circles, to portray a sense of order.)

Back at school children may like to add colour to their drawings, choosing colours that help convey the feeling of the subject matter. Explain how different colours reflect different moods, for example, red is often associated with feelings of anger.

Painting to music

Aim

To give children the opportunity to transmit their responses in a way other than words, and to think about how artists do this. This activity relates to the Art curriculum.

Age range

All ages.

Group size

Individuals and groups.

What you need

A museum display of abstract paintings or sculptures, large pieces of sugar paper, poster paints, brushes, recordings of distinctive or atmospheric music (for example: Jingle Bells, Greensleeves, 1812 Overture).

What to do

In the classroom, give each child three sheets of paper, brushes and poster paints. Explain that they are going to make three paintings of the same piece of music. Play the music once so they can hear it through, then three more times while they do three paintings – the first time, in one colour only, matching their arm movements and the lines made to the sounds; the second time making shapes suggested to them by the music; the third time mixing colours that the music suggests.

On the visit, look at abstract paintings and in groups talk about the three aspects above. If the paintings were music, what sounds would they be making?

Follow-up

On your return, the children could convert these paintings into musical sounds and then compose a piece to play on classroom musical instruments.

The postcard game

Aim
To familiarise pupils with specific works of art before a visit and to focus their attention on the detail once confronted with the real thing. This activity relates to the Art curriculum.

Age range
Seven to eleven.

Group size
Small groups.

What you need
A museum with a collection of prints and drawings, black and white postcards or photographs of the same works of art, scissors, paper, coloured pencils or oil pastels, envelopes.

What to do
Use postcards or photographs of works of art from the museum you are going to visit (obtain permission, if necessary, to take any photographs). Ideally they should be black and white renditions of coloured originals. Cut them up to make jigsaws (so that each child in each group will have a piece); it is not necessary for the pieces to interlink, so they can have straight sides. Ask the children to play with the jigsaws and piece them together. Swap the jigsaws round the class when they have been completed (use envelopes to keep the relevant pieces together).

Using a squared-grid and the usual scaling-up technique reproduce the jigsaw shapes on a much larger scale from plain paper; then cut them out. At the museum give each child one of the pieces of paper and the corresponding piece of original jigsaw picture.

At the museum ask each child to find the work of art that their jigsaw piece comes from. Then ask the children to copy the part of the work of art they have the jigsaw piece for. Tell them to try to record not just the colour but the textures too. If the jigsaw is in black and white and the work of art is in colour then they will be obliged to look very carefully in order to reproduce their piece.

In front of each work of art piece the children's drawings together on the floor and contrast the way each pupil has tackled their fragment of the work of art. Encourage the children to discuss the experience. What surprised them about their work of art? What had they liked? What had they discovered about the artist's method, colour range, intention? or whatever else might be appropriate.

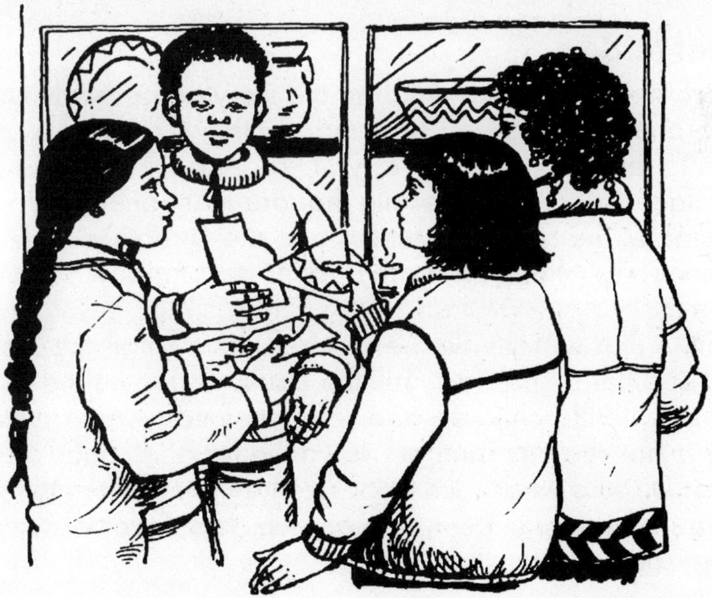

A Christmas story

Aim
To look at paintings of the Nativity. This activity relates to the RE and History curricula.

Age range
Five to seven.

Group size
Small groups.

What you need
A museum with paintings of the Nativity, pencils, paper and clipboards for the accompanying adults.

What to do
Before the visit tell the children the story of the Nativity from Luke, chapters one and two and Matthew, chapter two. Ask them to tell the story back to you. Together make a list of all the places, objects or people that are mentioned, such as the stable, the star, baby Jesus and the Three Kings. Make photocopies of this list for the adults accompanying you on the visit.

In the museum divide the children up in small groups to look at different pictures. Tell the adults to discuss the Nativity scenes with the children and see if they can work out what is or is not shown. Then go down the list and check off the items. Discuss what section of the story the artist is trying to make the viewer concentrate on; which point of view is being shown.

Follow-up
If the museum or gallery has other paintings of biblical themes (for instance Daniel in the lions' den, Joseph and his brothers and so on) you could look at these paintings before you leave and read the stories together back at school. The children could then draw or paint their favourite scene.

Landscapes

Aim
To introduce children to landscape paintings. This activity relates to the Art curriculum.

Age range
All ages.

Group size
Individuals.

What you need
A museum with four or five landscape paintings showing as wide a variety as possible, drawing paper, colouring materials such as wax crayons or pastels (not coloured pencils).

What to do
Look at the paintings you have selected and encourage the children to tell you what they can work out about such things as the time of day, weather, subject (wilderness or cultivation and so on) and intended mood. Ask them to tell you what sounds, temperatures, winds and so on are being indicated. Concentrate on having them imagine what it would feel like to be present in that setting.

Then ask pupils to choose a painting from those studied and do a coloured sketch including the main features only. When they return to school ask them to draw and colour the same scene in a different guise, for example changing the scene from stormy to peaceful, winter to summer. Ask them to concentrate on showing colours and lines that will make clear the mood of the scene. Repeat the exercise with another change of scene.

Display each child's favourite drawing. Ask them to write a descriptive piece to present near it, like a catalogue entry or a label.

Follow-up
Invite other members of staff or parents to a private viewing with the 'artists'.

Still life

Aim
To let children experience making a personal response to paintings, and to learn about their senses. This activity relates to the Art curriculum and to personal and social education.

Age range
Five to seven.

Group size
Small groups and individuals.

What you need
A museum with a selection of still life paintings showing flowers, fruit, animals, fish and so on, paper and clipboards for the accompanying adult, magazines with lots of coloured photographs, scissors and glue.

What to do
Divide the children up into small groups to look at the paintings. The adult with each group should ask the children to look at and list some of the things they can see in the painting, and give explanations if necessary. Then they should ask the children to close their eyes for a moment. They should try to remember what was in the picture as the adult asks them what they would be able to taste, touch, hear or smell. They should open their eyes and see if they can add anything to the list. Encourage the adults to linger over each sense and draw out as many 'sensations' as possible.

Back in school, give out the magazines, scissors, glue and paper. Ask the children to make their own still life by cutting out pictures and gluing them down. Each child should look for items which relate to one sense only, for instance things which would all have an interesting surface texture to feel or a noticeable scent to smell. Group their work into the appropriate sense and display it on the classroom wall.

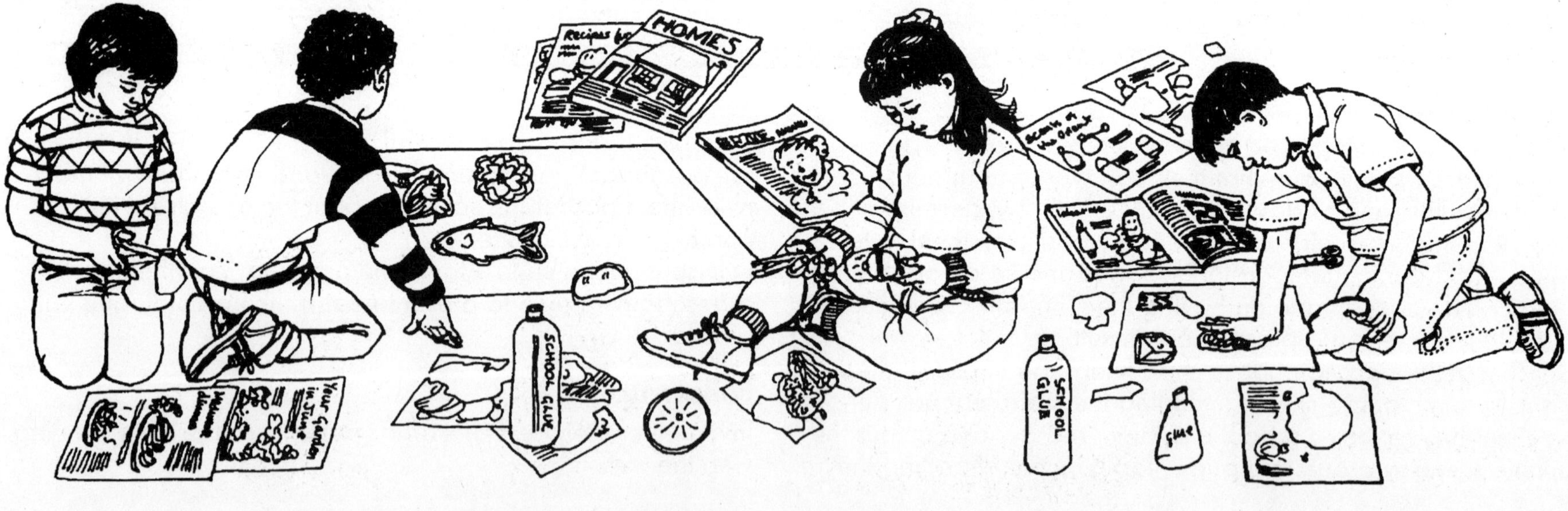

Sculpture

Aim

To show children that sculpture is often made to be looked at from all sides, not just the front. An object will differ in appearance depending on where you view it from and no one view is the 'true' view. This activity relates to the Art curriculum.

Age range

All ages.

Group size

Individuals.

What you need

A gallery with sculptures that you can walk all the way round, pencils, clipboards and paper or sketch-books. For the follow-up: modelling materials such as playdough or papier mâché.

What to do

In the museum settle the children on the floor in a circle round a sculpture that is intended to be seen from many angles. Ask them each to draw the sculpture exactly how it looks from where they are sitting.

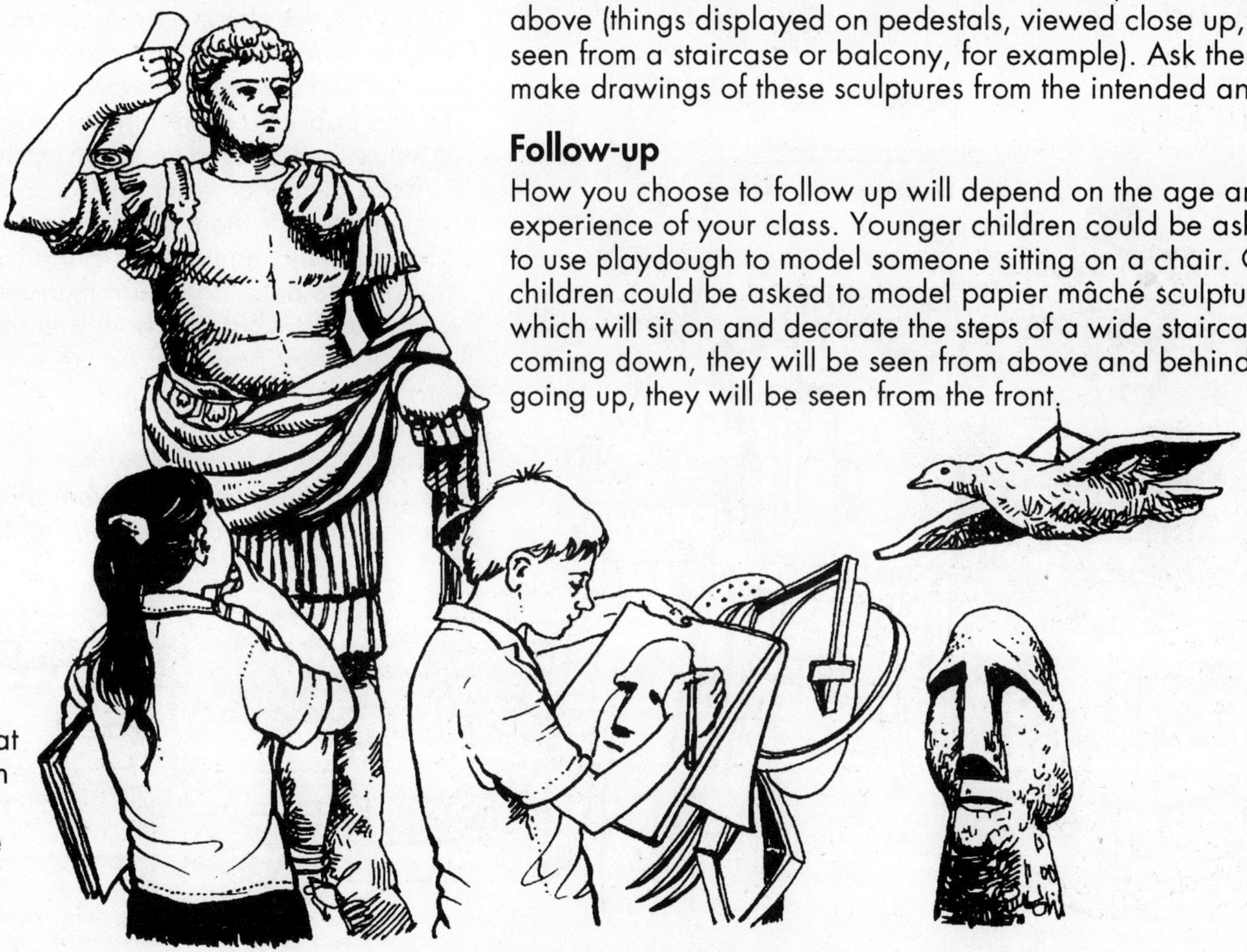

When the drawings are completed arrange them in a row on the gallery floor in the same order that the children sat in the circle. Discuss how the shape of the object gradually changes. Explain that sculptors have to consider what their work looks like from lots of different angles, not only from the front. Ask the children how successful they think the artist has been in making the work look interesting from all angles.

Now ask the children to see if they can find a sculpture that was intended to be looked at from below, or the side or above (things displayed on pedestals, viewed close up, or seen from a staircase or balcony, for example). Ask them to make drawings of these sculptures from the intended angle.

Follow-up

How you choose to follow up will depend on the age and experience of your class. Younger children could be asked to use playdough to model someone sitting on a chair. Older children could be asked to model papier mâché sculptures which will sit on and decorate the steps of a wide staircase – coming down, they will be seen from above and behind; going up, they will be seen from the front.

Plan an exhibition

Aim
To introduce the idea of an exhibition and how it is often based on a theme. This activity relates to the Art and English curricula.

Age range
All ages.

Group size
Small groups.

What you need
A museum with an art collection, clipboards, paper and pencils for the accompanying adults, art materials for use back at school.

What to do
This activity can be combined with any other at a museum. Once the other task has been completed ask the adults to spend a little time with the group discussing the displays. (How are the objects grouped? By theme, date or artist? If by theme, what themes have been chosen?) They should look out for and discuss the ways in which information is provided for the public. Together they should write a list of things that it would be useful to do when putting on an exhibition.

Back at school, each group should decide on a theme which interests them (or you can allocate a topic per group). They should refer to the list they made at the museum to help them plan their exhibition. They can decide who will do what and how it relates to the theme and then produce their paintings or art works. They should plan and produce an introductory panel which explains the exhibition's theme and make a heading banner that sums up the theme. Then individuals should write captions for their own work and mount the displays. Other classes could visit the exhibitions and put their comments in a visitors' book.

An 'artist's' book

Aim
To introduce the idea of a group-made book.
This activity relates to the Art curriculum.

Age range
Seven to eleven.

Group size
Whole class.

What you need
Any museum gallery, access to a photocopier, pencils, A4 paper, clipboards and art materials for use at school.

What to do
Note: the children should be made aware that the term 'artist' can refer to a poet, narrative writer, painter, etc. Explain to the children that some artists choose to make books which look beautiful. They are interested in the book as an object rather than as a narrative and so they feel the appearance is more important than words. A particular form of artist's book, which the children are going to make, is one made by several artists who each contribute sheets that are then bound together. These pages may be on a specific theme and include images or text or both. The artists will concentrate on the style of their sheet which will link in with the overall style and 'look' of the finished book. The content of their page, whether it be images or text, will reflect the overall 'feeling' of the book. (An example of this is the magazine *Verve* originated by Tériade, issued periodically between 1937 and the 1960s. Contributors included Matisse, Picasso and James Joyce.)

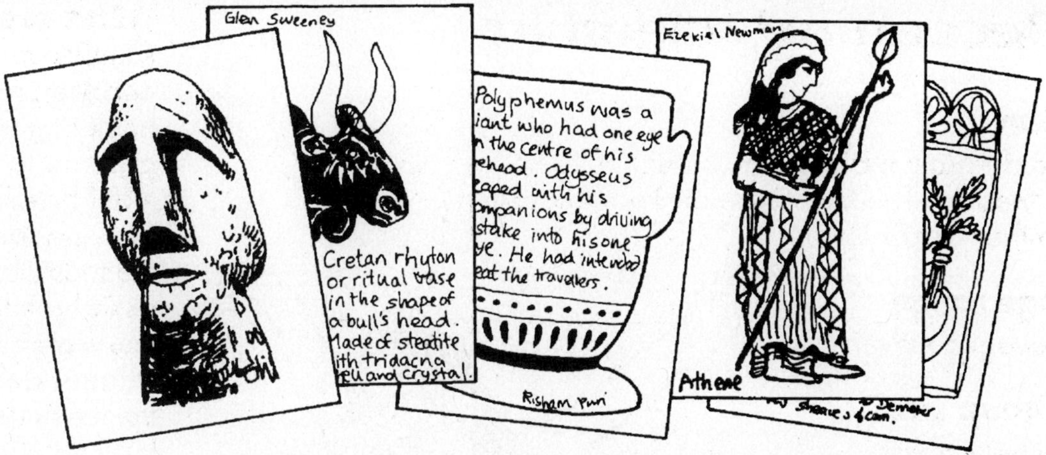

At the museum ask the children to work on a piece of art that represents the gallery to them. (Their work is to be in black and white only.) How you tackle this will depend in part on what art work they have done before. If they have done printing then you could ask them to record designs that might be converted into prints back at school. Some children might want to do detailed pencil drawings. Some might be interested in shapes and could record these ready to prepare a textured collage from which to make a rubbing. A gallery about another culture might have examples of scripts to record. Use the visit to allow the children to make notes, sketches and drawings that can be developed back at school.

At school pupils should aim to produce a completed piece of work in black and white on an A4 sheet of paper. If possible and relevant, allow pupils to make a photocopy of their work at an early stage. You will find that the photocopier improves the appearance of tentative pencil work and this is motivating for pupils who might then continue to develop their work by drawing on the photocopy.

Once the work is completed you can photocopy the pages so that all the children have a copy of the book and bind them using the Japanese method shown on page 21.

Decorating a teeshirt

Aim
To develop a design to use on a teeshirt. This activity relates to the Art curriculum.

Age range
Seven to eleven.

Group size
Whole class.

What you need
A museum collection such as ceramics, costume, wallpaper or tiles with surface decoration on, clipboards and paper or sketch-books, pencils, coloured pencils, sheets of cartridge paper, fabric crayons, scrap white fabric, white teeshirts and access to an iron.

What to do
Tell the children that you are going to be decorating teeshirts and that they should each bring into school a plain white one (with the permission of a parent or adult carer). It should be washed but does not need to be new.

At the museum ask the children to find some examples of motifs to use. They will need to make several very large drawings of these. The more stylised the motif the better it will work. Encourage pupils to record the colours used either in note form or by using coloured pencils.

Back at school demonstrate the fabric crayons by drawing sample patches, both even and uneven, on cartridge paper and then ironing them on to white scrap cotton fabric following the manufacturers' instructions. This will allow children to see the actual colours and effects. Using their motif drawings as inspiration, children should develop their designs so that they fill a panel that will fit on to the front of the teeshirt. When they are satisfied they should draw the design on to cartridge paper with a pencil and then go over the design with fabric crayons. It is important that this last stage is done accurately and evenly. Iron the pattern on to the teeshirts.

Follow-up
The class could put on a fashion show.

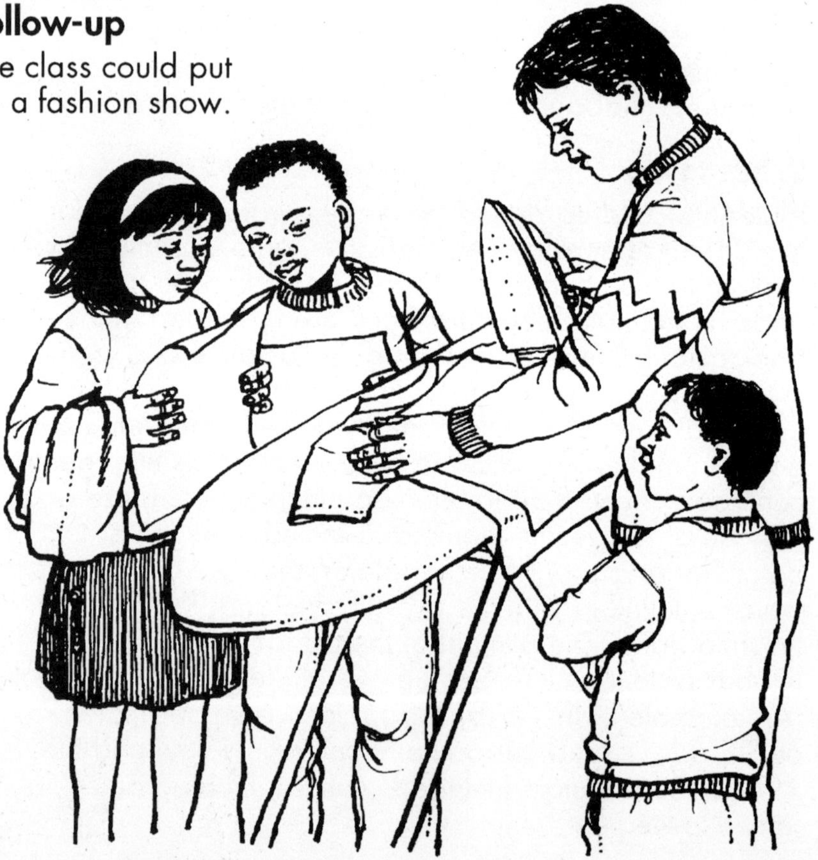

Hard looks

Aim

To help children appreciate that, in the past, delicate or complex objects were very costly because of the time they took to make. This activity relates to the Art curriculum.

Age range

Five to seven.

Group size

Individuals.

What you need

A museum collection with very intricate designs such as carpets, china decoration, silverware or costumes, sketch-books or paper and clipboards, pencils or coloured pencils.

What to do

In the museum tell children that they are going to undertake a challenge in patience and endurance. It will take time to achieve only a small amount, but the accuracy with which they work is important and those working fastest are probably doing least well.

Ask pupils to select an area of particularly detailed design on an object, and to copy it. Tell them to copy the work, making it larger: they can aim for twice life-size, which creates room for the details in the drawing. Tell them to do as much looking as drawing. Give them at least 15 minutes and ask them to produce their finest work. After this, they can swap and try another design.

Before you leave the museum make a display of the drawings on the gallery floor and find something good to say about each attempt. Ask whether it was easier to do the second drawing rather than the first? Ask pupils to tell you what they know about the stages which would have to be gone through and the methods used in the making of the objects. Can they estimate how much time it would take for one person to make the whole of one of the items they were drawing?

Ethnography

Telling a story

Aim

To introduce children to life in another culture. This activity relates to the English curriculum.

Age range

Five to seven.

Group size

Small groups and individuals.

What you need

A museum collection from the culture you are studying, clipboards, pencils and paper, coloured pencils.

What to do

Try to find a story about the culture you are studying that refers to the kind of objects that are in the museum. Tell the story to your class and explain that you are going to the museum to illustrate the story.

At the museum remind the children of the story and ask them to repeat it to you. Working in small groups with an adult to act as clerk the children should make a list of all the objects that appeared in the story. Then they should try and find them in the gallery. Tick the items off the list as they are found. Next ask the children to draw the objects and colour them. Back at school they should each draw a scene from the story using the pictures they drew at the museum to help them.

Making a story roll

Aim

To illustrate a story using a traditional Indian method. This activity relates to the English and Art curricula.

Age range

Seven to eleven.

Group size

Small groups.

What you need

A museum with a collection of Indian artefacts, sketchbooks, A4 paper, pencils, paints and brushes, a roll of paper 25cm wide by 2 metres long and glue.

What to do

Tell your class that they are going to tell stories in an Indian style. At the museum ask the children to research and record objects from India taking care to notice the colours that are frequently used. They should look for examples of cooking and eating utensils, clothing, jewellery, toys, tools and containers.

Back at school tell the class about Indian storytellers who travel round the villages with sets of story rolls. The story is illustrated by a series of pictures painted on a long paper roll. There is no text. The story teller sits in the centre of the village with the roll in his lap and the end thrown over his shoulder. He sings or chants the story, showing the appropriate pictures and passing the roll back over his shoulder as the action progresses.

Each group should invent a story incorporating some of the objects they have recorded. Talk with each group about their story and help them to develop it, if necessary. Divide the story into a number of scenes and make sure each child in the group has a scene to draw. Hand out sheets of A4 paper on which you have drawn identical borders and tell pupils they are to use it in landscape format. Decide together on the range of colours to be used. The rolls are more effective if the choices are limited. Once the groups have finished illustrating their stories paste each story together as a long roll and ask the groups to take it in turn to tell their story to the class.

Something to put it in: containers

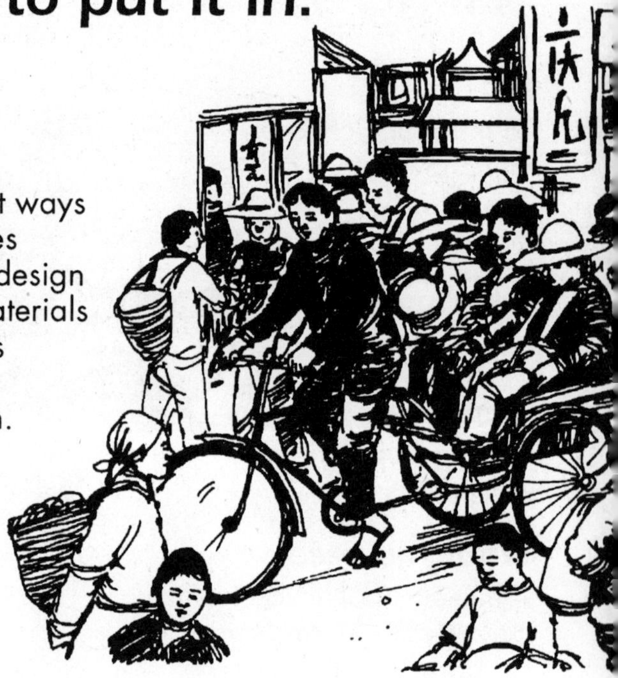

Aim
To look at the different ways people in other cultures have solved common design problems using the materials available to them. This activity relates to the Technology curriculum.

Age range
All ages.

Group size
Pairs.

What you need
A museum with an appropriate collection (for example: Japanese, Chinese or from an African tribe), sketch-books or clipboards and paper, pencils, glue, cardboard and string.

What to do
Ask children to look round the classroom and spot different containers. Discuss what they are made from, why they have been designed in that way and how effective they are for the job they are intended to do. Tell the children that they are going to study the containers made in another culture and then they are going to design their own.

Prepare the children for the containers they are going to see at the museum. In a Japanese collection, for example, there will be *inro* which are little boxes for holding small items that were attached to the sash around the middle of

the kimono. There may also be papier mâché picnic sets, games boxes or basketware containers for flowers.

At the museum ask pupils to record, through drawing or writing, the containers they see, noting what they have been made from, how they are secured and decorated, and what they are for. Help them to decide what factors have a bearing on function and decoration. Has the design been influenced by geographical location or by time?

Back at school pupils can be given the task of designing a container for a particular purpose using cardboard, glue and string. Some ideas might be: packaging for a present of 12 eggs, a container for a kettle or a telephone, a travelling container for a peacock, or box for a valuable ring that must be kept secure. They should prepare initial drawings before making their container. Ask the children to show their work to the rest of the class and explain their ideas.

Storing food: a technology project

Aim

To show that people living in other places face similar problems involving food storage as we do; to examine how these are solved with the technology available. This activity relates to the History, Geography and Technology curricula.

Age range

All ages.

Group size

Whole class.

What you need

A museum with a range of food storage items from one or several other cultures, pencils, paper and clipboards.

What to do

First discuss the following with the class: Why do you need to store food? What ways are there of preserving it? What are the threats to it?

In the museum look at different devices for storing food. Ask the children to draw them in detail. Help the children to start to classify them. Which are for dried food or for cooked food, for example? What materials are they made from? In what ways are they different from or similar to the methods used in the children's own homes?

Ask pupils which solutions they think might be most efficient for storing food. How well have the ideas been adapted for the resources that are available? How could they test their ideas without having access to the objects? Devise and carry out experiments to test these ideas and record the results.

The year in pictures

Aim

To make a study of how the seasons of the year influence the work and way of life in other cultures. At Key Stage 1 this activity relates to the History curriculum but at Key Stage 2 it fits better with the Art curriculum.

Age range

All ages.

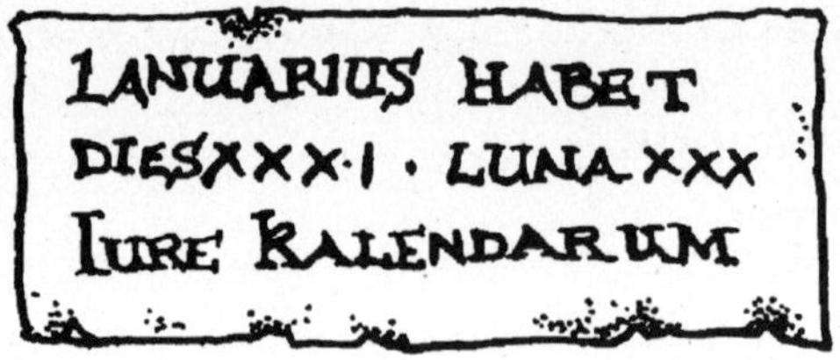

Group size

Small groups.

What you need

A museum with an appropriate collection, clipboards, pencils, paper, frieze paper, coloured pencils or paint, scissors and glue.

What to do

Depending on the culture being studied and the objects available to you it may be possible to get a picture of life during the different seasons of the year. Ask the children to research the details of the farming year and decide whether work differs according to the time of year. Choose appropriate seasons depending on the ability of the children: these could be Spring, Summer, Autumn and Winter, just Summer and Winter or you could choose the planting season and the harvest, for example.

In the museum the task is to try to find objects that are most likely to be used in their chosen season and to record them. Back at school the groups should produce a series of collages about each season. Alternatively, they could mime the use of their artefacts during the different seasons. For older children the exercise can be made more challenging by asking them to create drawings of scenes in the style of the culture being studied.

Maths from tiles

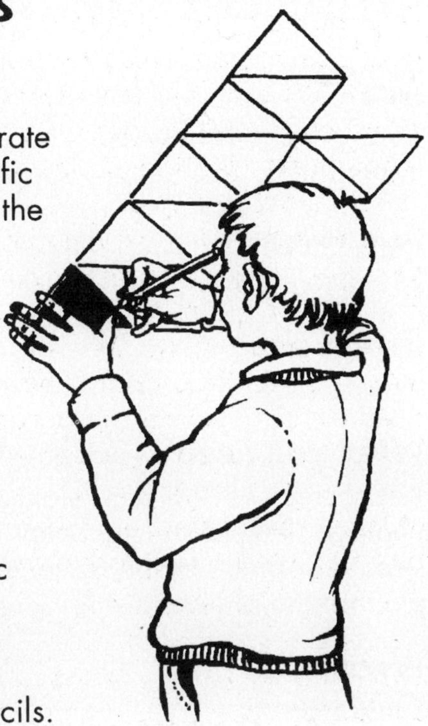

Aim
To use Islamic tiles to demonstrate symmetry, tessellation or specific shapes. This activity relates to the Maths curriculum.

Age range
All ages.

Group size
Individuals.

What you need
A museum collection of Islamic tiles, clipboards, pencils and paper, cardboard templates (page 120), isometric paper (page 121) and coloured pencils.

What to do
Start by assessing the tiles available to you. What are the mathematical possibilities? Are they simply square with a symmetrical pattern or are they varied in shape so that they tessellate in more interesting ways?

Before the visit make sure the children are familiar with shapes such as octagons, hexagons, squares, triangles, six-pointed stars and eight-pointed stars, and with the concept of symmetry. If you look at the patterns that are made you will find that they are either based on the number six or eight. For younger children shape recognition at the museum may be appropriate. Older children might be interested in investigating which sets of shapes always appear together.

Ask the children to try to reproduce some of the patterns. Give out the cardboard templates of the basic shapes for the children to draw round. (You could ask them to cut out the shapes from the sheet themselves at school, or you could do it.) At the museum ask them to record two or three different tessellations using the templates. Older pupils could be asked to copy designs on to paper. With designs based on eights this can be done on squared paper but those based on six will have to be done on isometric paper (see page 121). Pupils can be asked to develop their own coloured designs and those who think of themselves as 'no good at art' may be encouraged by the results.

Follow-up
If the tiles are square the children could make a set of paper tiles by drawing the squares on graph paper, cutting them out and then using them to record the designs on the tiles. Back at school ask pupils to make a set of four clay tiles with designs that fit together. Tell them to make some of the decoration in three dimensions and to colour the tiles to match each other.

Objects of faith 1

Aim

To show pupils how objects are used as aids to prayer in many faiths. This activity supports RE teaching.

Age range

Seven to eleven.

Group size

Whole class.

What you need

A museum with objects relating to prayer in any culture, photocopied sheets (see below) showing simple drawings of selected objects at the museum alongside a jumbled-up list of what the objects are for; clipboards, pencils and paper.

What to do

Ritual objects are usually only found in the relevant religious culture. Children often find them very interesting due to the great variety and their unfamiliar shapes. It may be possible to compare similar items from different faiths.

Many museums have objects and pictures related to Christianity such as altars, fonts, examples of clerical dress and church textiles, crosses and communion plates. Islamic items might include calligraphy, mosque lamps, fountains and carpets; you might also find Hindu, Buddhist, or Jewish items. Art galleries are likely to have altar pieces and nativity scenes.

Before the visit prepare and make photocopies of a sheet of simple drawings of objects related to prayer (that will be on display) alongside a jumbled-up list of what the objects are for. Discuss with the children the sorts of things that people through the ages and from different cultures have wanted to do or think about when praying. This might include concentrating on the deities they worship, remembering sets of particular words, or thinking about their own behaviour and ideas. Explain that some people want to go into a special place when they are praying, or surround themselves with a particular atmosphere, or show others that they are praying. Ask the children to give you examples from their personal or general knowledge of how these things are done.

In the museum, give the children the photocopied sheets. Ask them to find and name the objects, then match them up with the appropriate description. They should then write a few words suggesting how they think each object helps with the process of prayer.

This is an opportunity to invite local religious leaders either into the classroom or to join you on your visit to help explain and discuss more about the objects seen.

Objects of faith 2

Aim
To help children understand the part objects play in decorating places of worship. This activity supports RE teaching.

Age range
Five to seven.

Group size
Small groups.

What you need
A museum with objects which feature in places of worship of different cultures, pencils, coloured pencils, sketch-books or paper and clipboards.

What to do
In the museum, let the children look at the objects in small groups. Ask accompanying adults to talk with them about what the objects are and their function in the place of worship. Ask the children to look at and talk about how the items are decorated. For instance they may have precious stones and metals, pictures, patterns, rich colours or lots of different materials. Ask them to draw and colour the item they like the best.

Back at school, display the drawings and talk about why people make or give beautiful or costly objects to decorate their place of worship.

Mask 1

Aim
To produce a simple mask inspired by a museum visit. This activity relates to the Art and Technology curricula.

Age range
Five to seven.

Group size
Small groups and individuals.

What you need
A museum with a collection of masks, sketch-books or clipboards and paper, pencils, photocopiable sheet on page 122, thin card, scissors, coloured pencils or paint and brushes, decorative bits and pieces, a hole puncher or stapler and some thin elastic.

What to do
Before the visit check that your pupils have grasped the concept of masks. You could discuss a Guy Fawkes mask and talk about how masks were intended to hide the identity of the wearer, give a new identity, frighten or impress others in some way.

At the museum the children should go round in small groups with an adult and discuss the masks on display. These might be anything from a Venetian carnival mask to an African 'tree' mask, ritual masks or theatrical ones. What are they made of? Would they be heavy to wear? Which ones are frightening? Which ones are beautiful? Which do they like best? The children should draw some examples taking care to show the detail of the decoration.

Back at school give pupils a basic mask design photocopied on to card from page 122 and get them to cut it out (under supervision) and decorate it.

Follow-up
Pupils could use their masks when acting out a story you have told them recently.

Mask 2

Aim
To make a mask representing a particular culture. This activity relates to the Art curriculum.

Age range
Seven to eleven.

Group size
Individuals.

What you need
A museum with a collection of masks from a particular culture, clipboards and paper or sketch-books, pencils, clay, Vaseline, strips of newspaper, paste, brushes and paint and decorative material.

What to do
Tell the children that they are going to make a mask inspired by a particular culture. At the museum you can make sure that pupils study the full range of designs by asking them to look for and draw masks that might have served the following purposes:

• for an opera singer who would need her mouth uncovered.

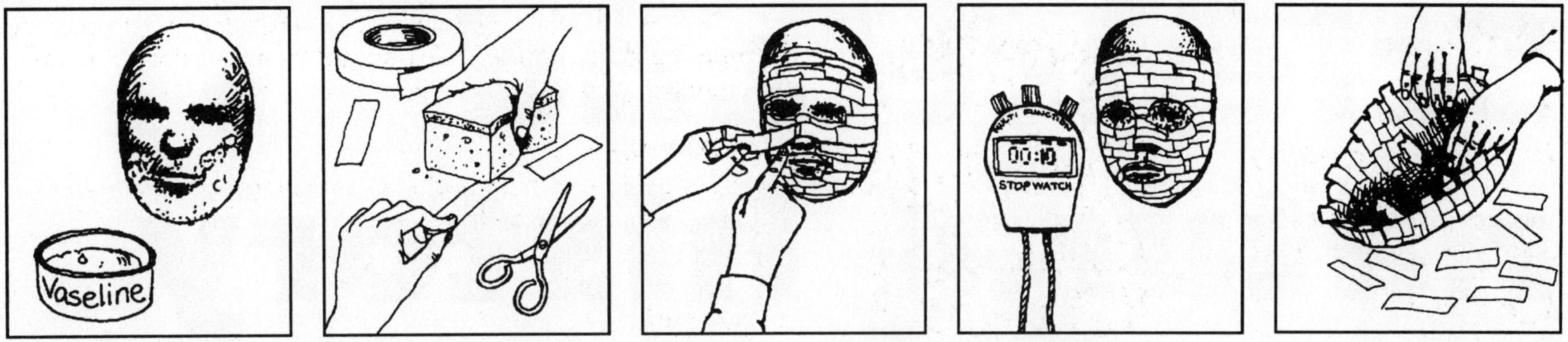

• for a character in a play who was very evil.
• for someone who was allergic to feathers and animal fur.
• for someone who wanted to show off their beautiful long hair while wearing the mask.
• for someone who wanted to hide their ears.

You can adapt this list depending on the special design features of the masks in the museum. When the drawings are completed discuss with the children the real purposes of the masks and the culture they come from.

Back at school tell the children how to make a mask. They should make a drawing of what they want to achieve and be able to say which of its features are inspired by the collection they have looked at in the museum. Using clay they should make a life-sized face shape on which to build their mask. Once the clay has dried smear it with Vaseline. Strips of torn newspaper soaked in paste should be pressed on to the shape until there is a reasonable thickness. Pay particular attention to the edges. Once this process is complete put the work aside to dry out. Lift the mask off and add further pieces of paste-soaked paper to patch up any weak parts – allow it to dry. Make holes for the eyes and mouth, and for the elastic which is to hold the mask in place.

Now ask the children to paint or decorate their mask in the style of the culture they have been studying. They may want to give it a coat of varnish.

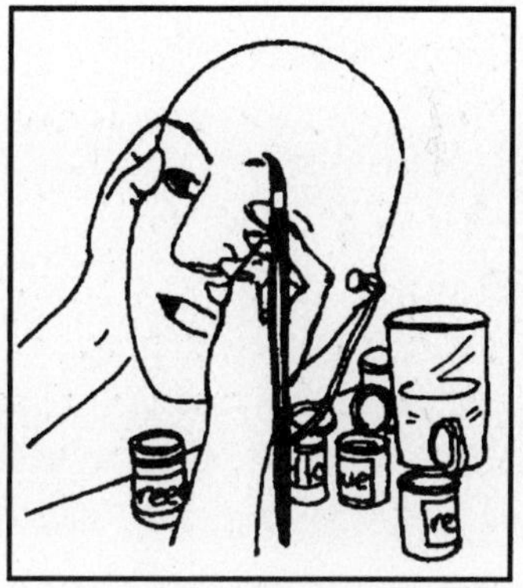

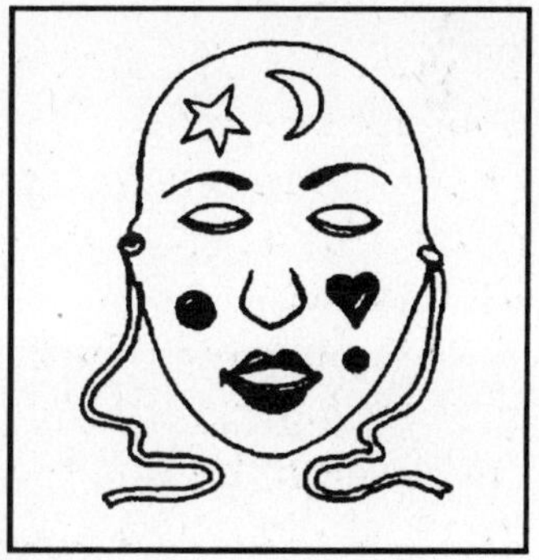

Science and natural history

A radio advert

Aim

To help children collect information from static displays and convert it into another format. This activity relates to the Science curriculum.

Age range

Five to seven.

Group size

Small groups and individuals.

What you need

A museum with cases of stuffed animals and birds, pencil, paper and clipboard for the accompanying adult and a hand-held tape recorder.

What to do

Tell the groups that their job is to examine the display cases, and produce a tape which could be used as a radio advert telling people what is in the museum and making them want to visit it.

At the museum, the adults should ask the group to study the animals in one case and suggest the sort of noises which might be heard in the wild. The adults should write down the suggestions which might include for instance, 'grass blowing in the wind', 'chewing noises'. (Avoid letting the children demonstrate noises loudly!)

Here is a list to go through. What sort of noises would be created by:

- the creature's voice;
- what the creature eats;
- how the creature moves;
- the environment in which it lives.

Make sure each child has a noise to make from the list. At school, with the help of an adult, the groups should think up a sentence which encourages people to come and see their exhibition case. Appoint one child to say this sentence. Remind the children of their noise and allow a little time for rehearsal. Then get the children to stand in a line. While you record each group at a time, each child in turn should make their noise, and the group's sentence should be read out by the appointed child.

Play back all the 'adverts' to the class and ask them whether the tape helped them to remember what they saw. How successful do they think the adverts are? Which case, other than the one they worked on, would they like to visit? What makes them interested in that particular case?

Life in a shoebox

Aim

To help children focus on the ways animals are adapted for their lifestyle. This activity relates to the Science curriculum.

Age range

All ages.

Group size

Individuals.

What you need

A museum with cases of stuffed animals and birds, drawing materials and clipboards, a shoebox (or similar) per child, scissors, glue, reference books and modelling materials.

What to do

In the museum, look at some examples of animals and birds and how they are adapted for their lives. For example look at:

- How their mouths are shaped to cope with what they eat.
- How their bodies have a covering to cope with where they live.
- How their feet are shaped to cope with how they need to move and where they live.
- How their bodies are shaped to cope with how they need to move.

You can also include any other features which seem apparent on the example you are showing, such as body size, position of eyes and so on.

Now explain that in order for the museum to preserve this important information about their specimens, and to make available material for other people to study, they want to make records of their exhibits. All the information for each animal must fit into a shoebox. Ask each of the children to choose one exhibit and make coloured drawings of the parts of the animal which show how they live (as in the above list).

Back at school give out the shoeboxes. Children must put in them as much information as possible about their animal. They can model, draw or paint various important parts such as the feet, the teeth or the type of skin. They can put in pieces of descriptive writing, drawings of paw prints and food, facts researched from library books, or even pictures cut out from magazines if available. The important thing is to try to build up a record of the animal from as many different sources as possible.

Decorate and label the shoeboxes on the outside. Let the class pass them round carefully, opening and looking at the contents. Ask individual children to make a presentation of the contents of their box, and what they found out that they think is especially important about their animal.

Rock identification

Aim

To help children practise observation and comparison. This activity relates to the Science curriculum.

Find a rock which you think could be used for:

- Decorating a crown
- A pavement
- Grinding up to make sand
- A very smooth table-top
- A statue
- Building a house

Age range

Five to seven.

Group size

Small groups.

What you need

A museum with displays of rock samples or mineral specimens, paper, pencil and clipboard for the accompanying adult, and a list made on your preliminary visit of the possible uses of rocks (see example on left).

What to do

Show the children the wide range of rocks that can be found, and ask them to suggest some of the differences – for example: there are bright colours, crystals, crumbly textures and hard, smooth rocks. Give the groups a list like the one shown, and ask them to find and record the names of rocks that they think could be useful for the purposes given. At the end, find out which rocks they chose and why.

Cars

Aim

To help children compare transport now with transport in the past, and to think about change through time. This activity is based on cars but, depending on the collection, you could base it on trains or bicycles instead. The activity relates to the History curriculum.

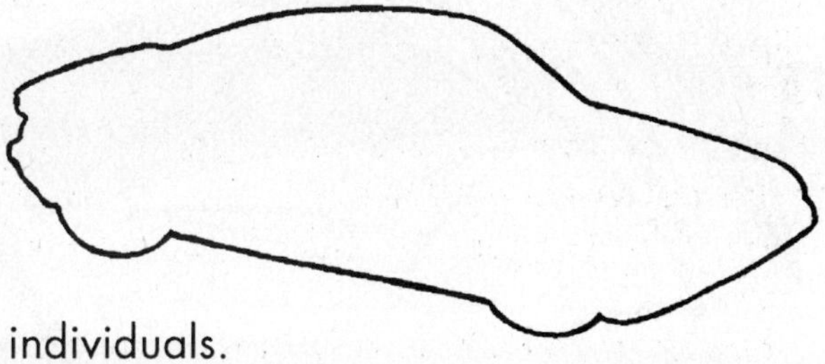

Age range

All ages.

Group size

Whole class and individuals.

What you need

A museum with cars on show (ideally three different examples to compare), simple card templates giving the basic outline of the cars in the museum, scissors, glue, pencils, paints and magazines or books showing pictures of modern cars.

What to do

At the museum, walk round the site and look at your chosen examples starting with the oldest. At each one, look for the same basic features so that you can see how they alter, for instance, how the driver gets in and sits, the type of wheels, how the doors fasten, how you get at the engine. Draw comments and observations from the children about these.

Back at school, let children draw round the templates of the cars, then fill in the rest of the details and paint them. They can cut the cars out and fix them on the wall, grouped according to age. Finally, let the children cut out and stick up some pictures of modern cars next to the older ones. You could show them some prototypes and then, as a group, talk about how cars might change in the future.

Dinosaurs at large!

Aim

To help children think about how different dinosaurs were adapted for their environments. This activity relates to the Science curriculum.

Age range

Five to seven.

Group size

Individuals.

What you need

A museum with dinosaur skeletons, fossils and/or dioramas, some plastic models of different types of dinosaurs – enough for each child to have one (some can be duplicates; you need actual dinosaurs, not imaginary ones; you also need ones that appear in the museum displays), a classroom sand tray, a sticky label on each dinosaur giving its name, an aquarium with a little water in, a washing line across the classroom and thread.

What to do

Give each child a labelled dinosaur and tell them how to say the name. Take the dinosaurs to the museum. Let the children look at the displays and help them to find information about their dinosaur. They should find out whether it was usually found on land, in the sea or in the air. (Some may have been found in a combination of these.)

Back at school, hold up different dinosaurs in front of the class and ask their owners to point out some clues on the body which reflect the dinosaur's lifestyle. Ask the children to place the land-living dinosaurs in the sandtray and the water-living dinosaurs in the aquarium. Help the children with flying dinosaurs to tie thread round them and suspend these in flight from the washing line.

Alternatively: ask children to paint a background scene for their dinosaur. Pin up all the water-scenes side by side and arrange the dinosaurs in front of them; then all the land scenes and so on, to make a panoramic frieze along the classroom wall.

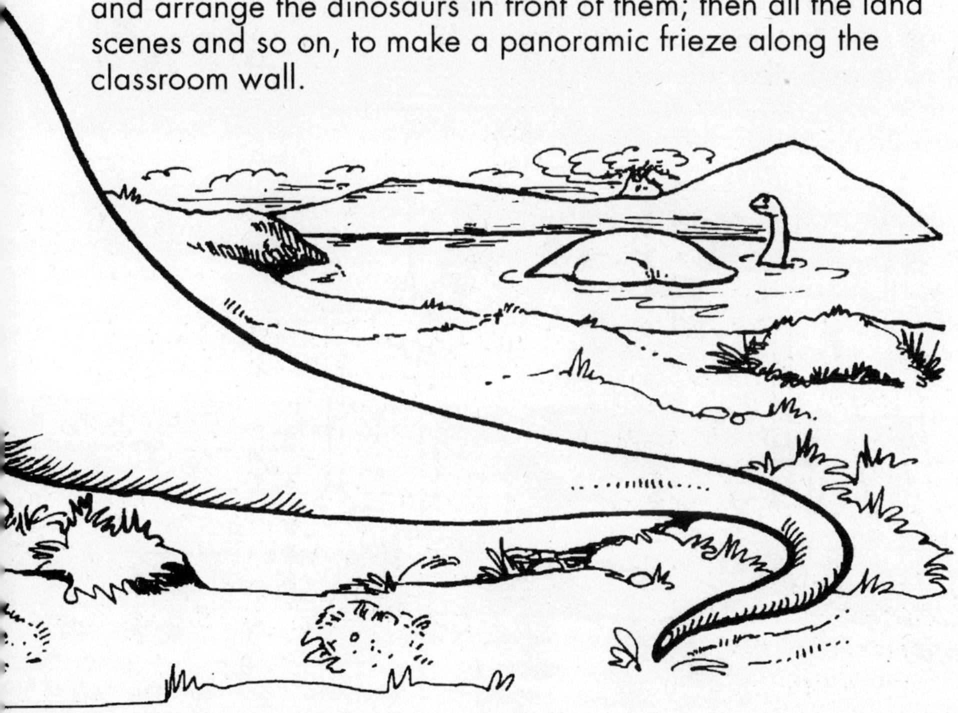

A weather vane

Aim

To help children think about the work of people in a rural agricultural society. This activity relates to the History and Geography curricula.

Age range

Seven to eleven.

Group size

Individuals.

What you need

A museum with agricultural implements and objects, paper, pencils and clipboards, large yoghurt or cream pots with lids, dry sand or gravel, long pencils or old knitting needles to use as the spike, page 123 copied on to thick card (one for each child), black and white paint, transparent tape and a compass.

What to do

In the museum, ask children to look for and list and/or sketch items that they think might have been found in the lives of a landowner, a labourer and a farmer's wife or dairymaid. Gather the class together and ask them what items they have found, and what these do.

Hand out the card copies of the activity sheet. Ask the children to draw on the weather vane a simple outline (silhouette) showing one of the characters above holding or using a piece of the equipment that the children have discovered their character would have used.

Back at school, tell the children to cut out their weather vanes and paint the pots and their lids black. Then they can paint the silhouetted person on the weather vane black and the surrounding area white (if you are very ambitious and have enough time you could cut out the silhouette with a craft knife). Ask them to trace the silhouette, turn the card over, transfer the drawing on to this side and paint again. Tape the weather vane to a pencil with the point down. Fill the pots with well-packed sand and tape the lids on very firmly. Turn them upside down. Stab the pencil point carefully through the pot and settle it well in making sure that the weather vane can swivel. Mark N, S, E and W on the top of the pot around the pencil.

On a dry day take the weather vanes outside and line them up with the compass points (choose a relatively open area where the wind is not gusting, for example, not in alleys between buildings). When the wind comes from the North, the arrow point of your weather vane should point to the North. Ask the children to take readings every thirty minutes throughout the day to see how the wind changes.

In role: farmer's merchant

Aim
To encourage children to look at a range of unfamiliar tools. This activity relates to the Technology curriculum.

Age range
Seven to eleven.

Group size
Pairs.

What you need
A museum with displays of agricultural implements, the text below, clipboards, pencils, coloured pencils and paper.

What to do
At the museum give this text to each pair and ask them to respond.

Back at school the children should complete their catalogues and then discuss which three tools they think will be the best sellers. This is an open-ended activity which can be as simple or complicated as suits the time you have available.

'You are a Victorian merchant dealing in tools and equipment for farmers. You have decided to go into the mail order business. Prepare a catalogue of your products with short descriptions to explain clearly what each tool does and how they will help the farmer at work.'

Haiku

Aim
To use a museum visit to encourage creative writing. This activity relates to the English curriculum.

Age range
Seven to eleven.

Group size
Individuals and pairs.

What you need
A museum collection of natural history objects, clipboards, coloured pencils, pencils, paper.

What to do
Discuss haiku in class. Haiku are poems with 17 syllables. They have three lines with five syllables in the first, seven in the second and five in the last. The concept comes from Japan and the traditional subject is nature. Haiku are usually about the feelings of the moment, focusing on what caused the emotion rather than the emotion itself. Judgemental words should be avoided.
Here is an example:

Peering at the stars
Through its gaps between branches
The lovely willow
Miura Chora (1729-80)

At the museum ask pupils to spend some time looking at the collection and writing notes about what they see, hear or feel. They should write down anything that floats into their minds but try to keep concentrating on the collection. After five to ten minutes ask pupils to sit down and write a haiku. Read out some of the work in front of the objects to which they refer.

Back at school pupils should work in pairs, listening to each other's work and revising it. Remind them of the rules above. Once they are happy with their poems, they could go on to illustrate them. Perhaps they could then make up some other poems relating to a favourite topic, for example, a favourite toy or television programme. Make a book with a Japanese binding to hold the class's work (see page 21).

Industrial espionage: using a secret code

Aim

To widen children's understanding of how changes in technology can be the result of closely guarded work and ideas. The activity uses a secret code to provide some excitement and show that people have not always wanted to share their ideas. This activity relates to the History and Technology curricula.

Age range

Seven to eleven.

Group size

Pairs.

What you need

A museum with a collection of inventions or a range of items showing technological innovation, a decoder (see page 124 – enlarge if necessary), pencils, sketch-books or paper and clipboards, ruler, scissors and cardboard.

What to do

Before the visit tell the children what you are going to study and discuss with them why some people might not want to share new ideas. Objects in museums can often help when looking at technological change. How were tools in the Stone Age different from tools produced in the Iron Age? What changes took place in the organisation of industrial production in the Industrial Revolution? How was women's work different in the nineteenth century from the 1930s?

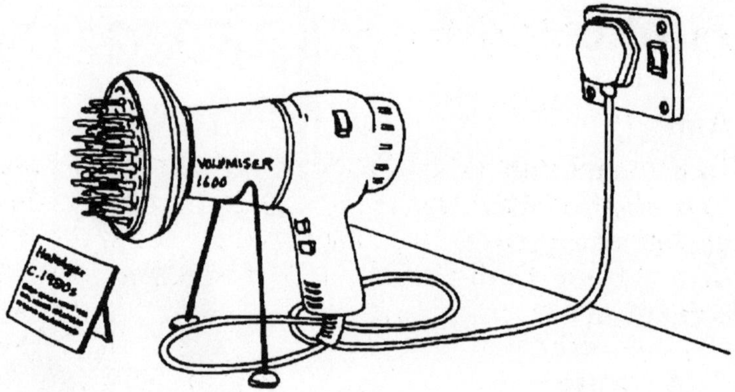

Choose the museum and your topic depending on your curriculum needs.

Ask the children to pretend that they are spies being sent out to gather information. They are going to have to send a report back about their findings in code. Give out copies of page 124 and help them to make their decoders. They will have to cut out the main shape and the alphabet strip. Then they cut two small slits for the alphabet strip to be pulled through. Show the children how to convert their message into code by using the two alphabets on their decoder. Explain that one should start with A and the other, starting with any letter, should fall exactly below – once the end of the alphabet on the strip is reached then the remaining spaces are filled by starting at the beginning. If the letter below A is an R the code is known as an R alphabet or if it is a C then it is a C alphabet. Any coded message should start with the letter for the alphabet name and thereafter the original letters are substituted with their code equivalent.

At the museum pupils should make sketches and notes on their discoveries. Back at school pupils should prepare their messages and write titles and captions for their diagrams in code too, using their decoder. One pair can swap messages with another pair. Once the message is deciphered they can discuss their findings.

A zoetrope

Aim

To show that some toys work through the application of a scientific principle and that moving images can be created by showing a changing picture faster than the brain can take in the individual drawings. This activity relates to the Science curriculum.

Age range

Seven to eleven.

Group size

Whole class.

What you need

A museum with a zoetrope that you can demonstrate, a round biscuit tin and an improvised stand, a strip of paper (per child) about 7cm wide and long enough to fit all the way round the inside of the tin, pencils and coloured pencils or felt-tipped pens.

What to do

At the museum show your class a zoetrope. Place a printed strip inside the drum and spin it. Let the children look through the slits so that they can see the drawings move. The pictures are usually of things such as acrobats somersaulting, birds flying and fish swimming. Once pupils have seen one of these toys in action they will easily understand the principle. The strip has a series of drawings in slightly different positions and the showing of each drawing in quick succession makes the brain think the picture is moving.

Back at school enlist the help of an adult to make the barrel of your zoetrope from a large round biscuit tin and improvise a central stand.

Give your pupils long strips of paper and ask them to decide what moving thing they want to show. They should then plan and draw a series of pictures so that by the end of the paper that movement has been completed. Pin figures will work very effectively. Test in the zoetrope and adjust if necessary. When the children are satisfied with their drawings they can colour them with felt-tipped pens, keeping identical colours in each of the drawings of the series.

Discuss the scientific principle that this demonstrates and how the idea led on to the idea of the cinema.

Stopping and starting a bike

Aim

To show the simple principles on which a bicycle works. This activity relates to the Technology curriculum.

Age range

Seven to eleven.

Group size

Individuals and small groups.

What you need

A museum with a collection of bicycles of different ages, a bicycle belonging to a member of the class, pencils, reference books, sketch-books or clipboards and paper.

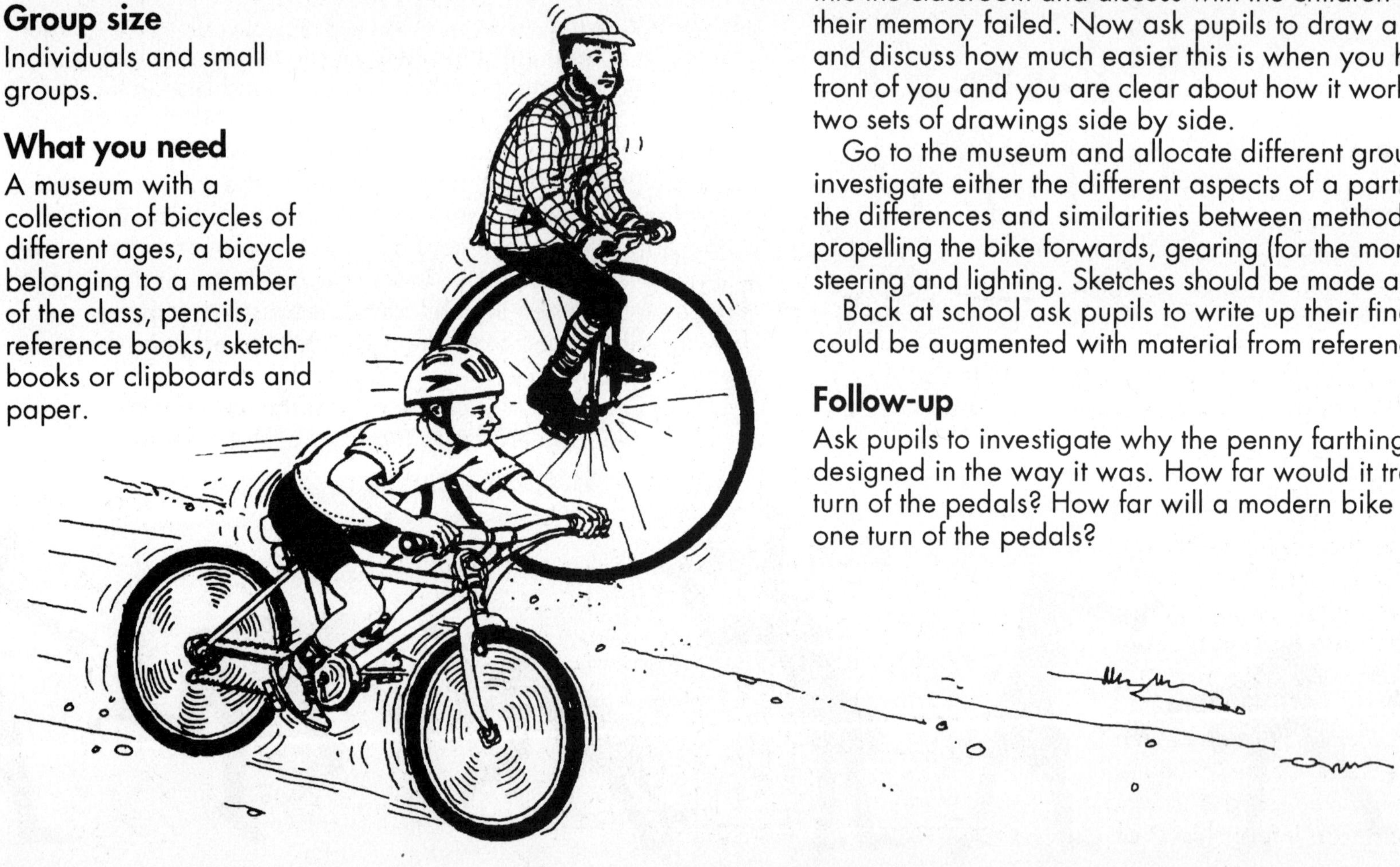

What to do

At school discuss with your class what they know about bicycles. Most pupils will have their own or have learned to ride on someone else's. You can capitalise on this and their prior knowledge of how a modern bike functions.

Ask pupils if they can draw a bicycle. Get them to do so and you will find that earlier confidence diminishes as they struggle to remember the relationship of the various parts. Keep these drawings then ask someone to bring their bicycle into the classroom and discuss with the children the bits where their memory failed. Now ask pupils to draw a bicycle again and discuss how much easier this is when you have one in front of you and you are clear about how it works. Display the two sets of drawings side by side.

Go to the museum and allocate different groups to investigate either the different aspects of a particular bike or the differences and similarities between methods of braking, propelling the bike forwards, gearing (for the more advanced), steering and lighting. Sketches should be made as appropriate.

Back at school ask pupils to write up their findings which could be augmented with material from reference books.

Follow-up

Ask pupils to investigate why the penny farthing was designed in the way it was. How far would it travel with one turn of the pedals? How far will a modern bike travel with one turn of the pedals?

Keeping the door shut

Aim

To investigate a simple technological problem for which there are a number of possible solutions. This activity relates to the Technology curriculum.

Age range

Seven to eleven.

Group size

Individuals.

What you need

A museum with a collection of doors, cupboards and boxes that need to be kept shut (and ideally a display of locks), clipboards, pencils and paper.

What to do

Tell pupils that you are going to study the way people in the past or in other cultures have fixed doors shut. Pupils could start off in the school and see what variants they can find. Help the children classify the solutions. How many doors can only be fixed from one side? How many can be fixed from both sides? Are there any that can be shut from both sides but only locked from one side? How have these different problems been solved?

Continue the study at the museum. Are different materials used and if so why? Is the fixing an integral part of the door or is it done by a separate part? Are there any new methods on display at the museum? Make sure children record their findings.

Follow-up

This will be determined by the collections you have been looking at. It may be appropriate to make some models of some of the devices that have been seen; or you may want to set a problem asking pupils to design a particular type of door closure, for example: one for a door that can be opened all day from either side but that needs to be locked from the inside at night and there is only wood available to work with.

Any collection

A present for a queen, a baby...

Aim

To help children start to look at objects analytically, identify the purpose of the object and to acquire a sense of its status. This activity relates to the English curriculum.

Age range

Five to seven.

Group size

Small groups.

What you need

Any museum.

What to do

This is a very general activity suitable for a first visit to a museum. Working in small groups with an adult ask the children to look at the objects on display and say which they would choose, and why, as a present for various people. The adult should have a list of varied people such as a queen, your granny, a baby, dad, the head teacher, a nurse or the milkman to prompt them. They can help the children discuss how you tell the difference between an object intended for a rich person and one for a poor person; an object for public display and so on.

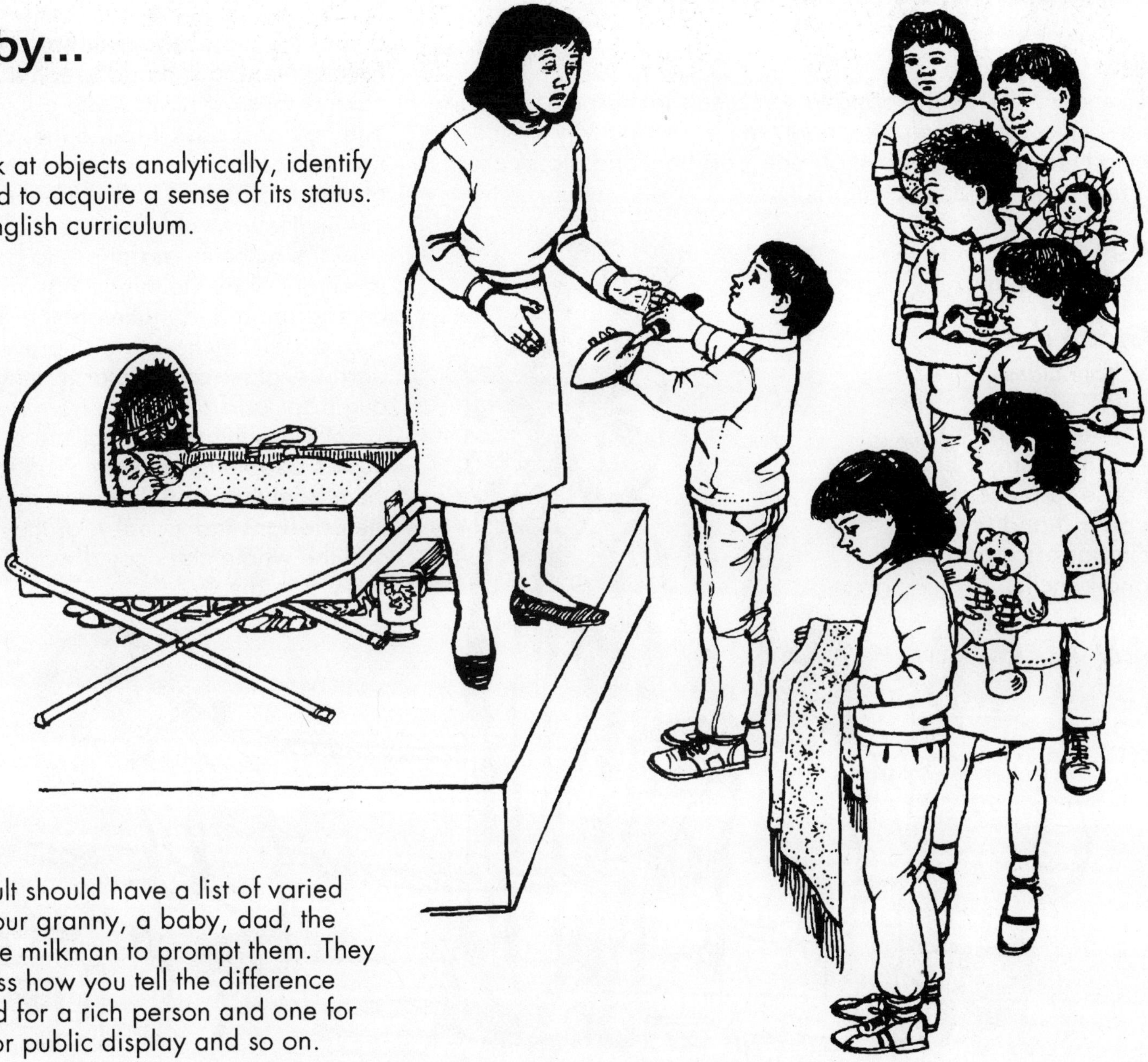

Conserving the objects

Aim

To show children the dangers to objects in museums and how museums attempt to protect them. This activity should help them to see the point of ropes, barriers and glass cases. It relates to the Science curriculum.

Age range

Seven to eleven.

Group size

Whole class.

What you need

Any museum or historic house, a piece of white paper, hand mirrors, clipboards, paper and pencils.

What to do

In school explain the term 'conservation' and that in museums one of the most serious threats to the objects is the visitors. People need to see and breathe, and they touch things. Take a sheet of plain white paper and cut it in half. Take one half and pass it round the whole class. Compare the two pieces and discuss how handling it for that short space of time has altered it. Breathe on a mirror and ask what the mist is. How would dampness affect objects?

At the museum ask pupils to go round and make an inventory of all the things that are showing signs of deterioration and make another list of all the things that curators are trying to do to prevent this. Include ropes and barriers, glass cases, plastic screens, temperature control, bug traps and protection from damp.

Back at school ask pupils to design a museum gallery that allows people to get very close to the objects but protects them from the main threats. If there is time, they could model their designs individually, or they could choose one design and the whole class could work together to produce a classroom display.

A visitor survey

Aim
To teach children a method of acquiring information and to reinforce maths activities. This activity relates to the Geography and Maths curricula.

Age range
Seven to eleven.

Group size
Small groups.

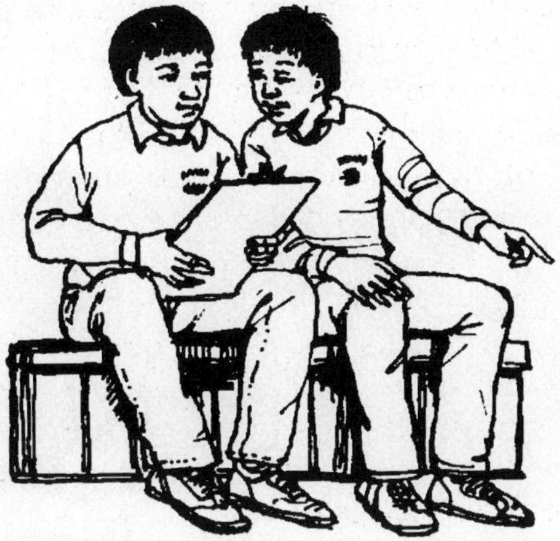

What you need
Any site or museum, photocopied sheets from pages 125 and 126, pencils, paper and clipboards.

What to do
You should get the permission of the museum before embarking on this activity. Tell the children that they are going to find out who visits the museum. Discuss how museums are very interested in the types of people who visit them. They want to know what proportion of their visitors are family groups and what proportion are tourists or foreign visitors. They also want to know where people have come from and how far they have travelled, whether they have come before and how they enjoyed their visit. This information can be used to help improve museums or to plan marketing campaigns.

Explain to the children that they are going to find out some of this information for themselves. They should sit where they can see the entrance and record the size of groups that arrive and their 'make up'. Then they can track a party round a gallery recording the places where people stop and the objects they look at or the labels they read. They could record the amount of time that people spend in specific galleries. They could record the decisions people make about where to go when they arrive in the entrance hall of the museum.

If you feel this part of the activity might not be practicable (to track one party), the different groups could sit in different parts of the gallery and observe (from afar) what people look at. Then the groups could come together and collate their information.

Ask the children to conduct some visitor interviews. Make up your own questionnaire or photocopy the one on page 125. You will need to ensure that the children operate in groups of three or four and understand the rules of personal safety and politeness.

Back at school the information can be translated into bar charts, pie charts and line graphs. They could use page 126 to record diagrammatically how far visitors have travelled (the distance travelled has been represented by a series of concentric circles) by translating the information they obtained regarding travel on their visitor survey sheet on to this travel survey sheet.

A trail for blind people

Aim

To show children that there are ways of experiencing the museum other than simply by sight. This activity relates to the English curriculum.

Age range

Seven to eleven.

Group size

Small groups.

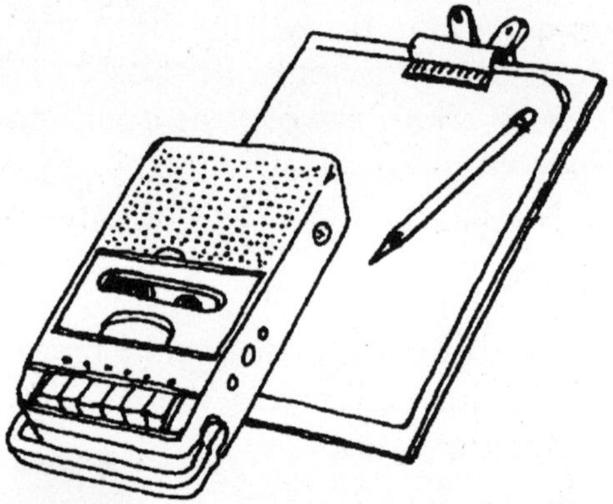

What you need

Any museum, clipboards, pencils, paper and a tape recorder.

What to do

Tell your pupils that they are going to visit a museum and then prepare a trail for a blind person. First go to the museum and prepare carefully. Find out whether there are areas where you can touch objects – will your pupils be able to plan a touch tour or will they have to rely on other senses? Choose small areas of the museum for pupils to work in groups. Select areas where people can touch objects; where there are interesting things to describe; where routes can be followed by use of handrails or floor texture; where noises or smells can be utilised.

On the visit give pupils time to have a general look round and then ask them to work in the selected areas. Get them to discuss how they could make use of the material there. If you have a collection of hand-held tape recorders then pupils could use these to record their trails. They could swap their work and try out each other's activities. If there is only the use of one tape recorder, the groups could take turns to record their routes and then follow each other's recorded routes (on the same day or on another visit to the same museum).

Schools with contact with visually impaired people could ask them to discuss what things they would find most helpful and what things make life awkward.

A guidebook for a museum

Aim
To make children analyse what they want to say and think how to organise information. This activity relates to the English curriculum.

Age range
Seven to eleven.

Group size
Small groups.

What you need
Any museum with display cases containing over five objects, clipboards, pencils and paper.

What to do
In class discuss the purpose of guidebooks. You might look at some examples. Discuss how information is given through text, illustrations and captions to those illustrations. Tell the children they are going to a museum to write sections of a guidebook. Try to set a question for each group. If you knew one group, for example, was going to get a display case containing 20 Chinese pots to work on then the question might simply be 'What were the main kinds of decoration on Chinese pottery?'; or if they were to get a case of Roman craft tools the question could be 'What did the Romans make and how?' These kind of questions will help pupils to develop a structure.

At the museum pupils should have a general look round and then each group should work on their case. Encourage drawing and ask for captions for all illustrations (written with the question in mind).

Back at school pupils can complete their work and the sections can be put together to form a book. This kind of activity might benefit from being set again in another gallery on another topic so as to draw on previous experience.

Anytown Museum

Date

Acme Picture Postcard Company
Some Street
Shireford

Dear Sir

Anytown Museum needs to extend its range of picture postcards and we would like you to visit the museum and make some recommendations. We would like you to start with our Tudor galleries. Assume that we have no cards already on this subject. We would like you to decide which six objects best represent the galleries. Please prepare sketches to show us what you are proposing and write the line of descriptive text that normally goes on the back of the postcard. We would like a brief covering letter explaining why you made your selection.

We look forward to hearing from you with your proposals,

Yours faithfully

Curator

In role: the Acme Picture Postcard Company

Aim

To make children look generally at a gallery or area of the museum and establish their own criteria for selection. This activity relates to various areas of the curriculum.

Age range

Seven to eleven.

Group size

Pairs.

What you need

Any museum collection, sketch-books or clipboards and paper, pencils.

What to do

The following activity is very flexible as it can be used at most galleries, museums or sites. You have to decide what it is you want your pupils to focus on and make that the subject of the task.

Ask pupils to work in pairs in the gallery and give them the letter (to the left) adapted as appropriate.

It is very important that you get pupils to work together on this type of activity as the discussion is as important as the final outcome. Pupils may find making their own decisions hard initially and will probably need practice.

Poster to advertise the museum

Aim

To produce a poster to advertise a museum showing the range of items on display. This is a whole class activity and can be used to discuss the role of museums. The activity relates to the Art curriculum.

Age range

All ages.

Group size

Whole class.

What you need

Any museum, pencils, sugar paper, large sheets of drawing paper, art materials for use in class.

What to do

Divide a large sheet of drawing paper into enough equal spaces for each child to have one piece. (Depending on the size of the class, you may need to divide more than one sheet.) At the museum give out the pieces of paper and allocate each child a letter of the alphabet. Ask them to find and make a sketch of an object beginning with that letter. They should also find out about museum opening times and admission costs.

Back at school, ask the children to finish off their drawings. Mount a large piece of sugar paper (large enough to make a frame around the drawings). Have a discussion with the class to decide where each drawing should be placed according to certain criteria – different exhibitions, periods, or objects could be put together.

Then get the children to paste their drawings on to the sugar paper. Discuss with the children why people advertise. To finish the poster off, add the opening times and admission costs in an appropriate space and put a heading with the title of the museum above the poster so that visitors will know what the poster relates to.

Reproducible material and resources

Looking at an object: analysis form, see page 24

What does it look like?	What is it made from?	How was it made?	What was it for?	What does it tell us?

Finding out about history from an object, see page 24

What does the object look like?

What is it made from?

How was it made?

What was it made for?

Why does it look like it does?

When was it made? (Use the museum label to find a date or a period.)

Who do you think made it?

What do you think it tells us about the person who made it?

Who do you think used it?

If this was a different person from the person who made it, what do you think it tells us about the user?

What does this object tell us about the time in which it was made?

What else do you think you need to know about it?

Finding out about design from an object, see page 24

What does the object look like?

What is it made from?

What is it made for?

Why has it been made as it is?

Does it do the job it was designed for?

Can you think of ways of improving it?

Do you like it? Why?

Diagrams 1: using charts, see page 26

Diagrams 2: using Venn diagrams, see page 27

Looking at the archaeological evidence, see pages 29 and 32

The period I am studying is ____________

What I can say for certain	Evidence

What I think was the case	Evidence

What I don't know	How I could find out

How to find the circumference of a pot from a piece of rim, see page 31

Hold up the piece of rim against the lines until you find the one that matches. Then you can read off the diameter of your pot. Make sure you hold the rim flat – do not tilt it. Now you can find the circumference of your pot.

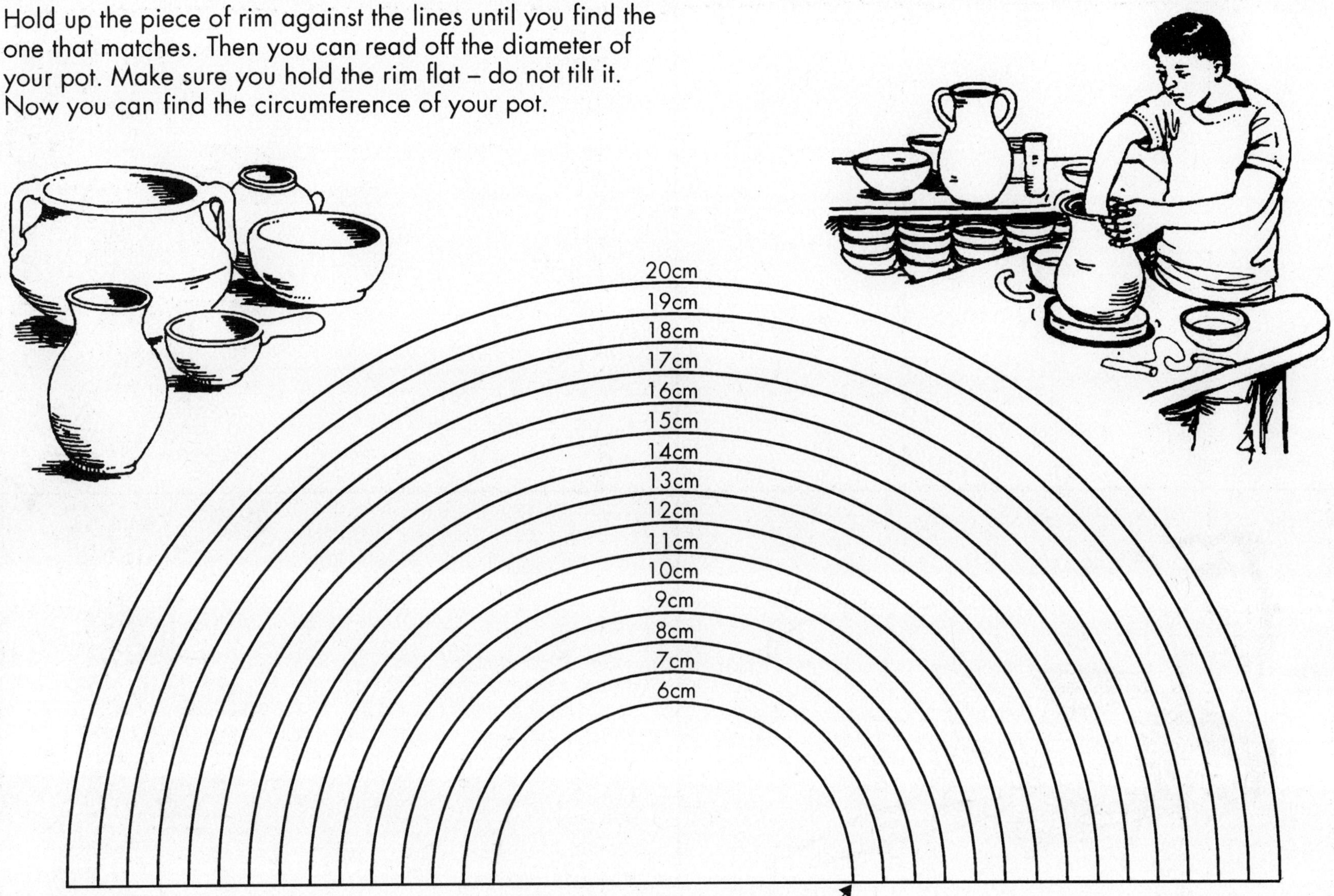

If your fragment fits this line, your pot has a diameter of 6cm.

How to draw an Ancient Egyptian, see page 40

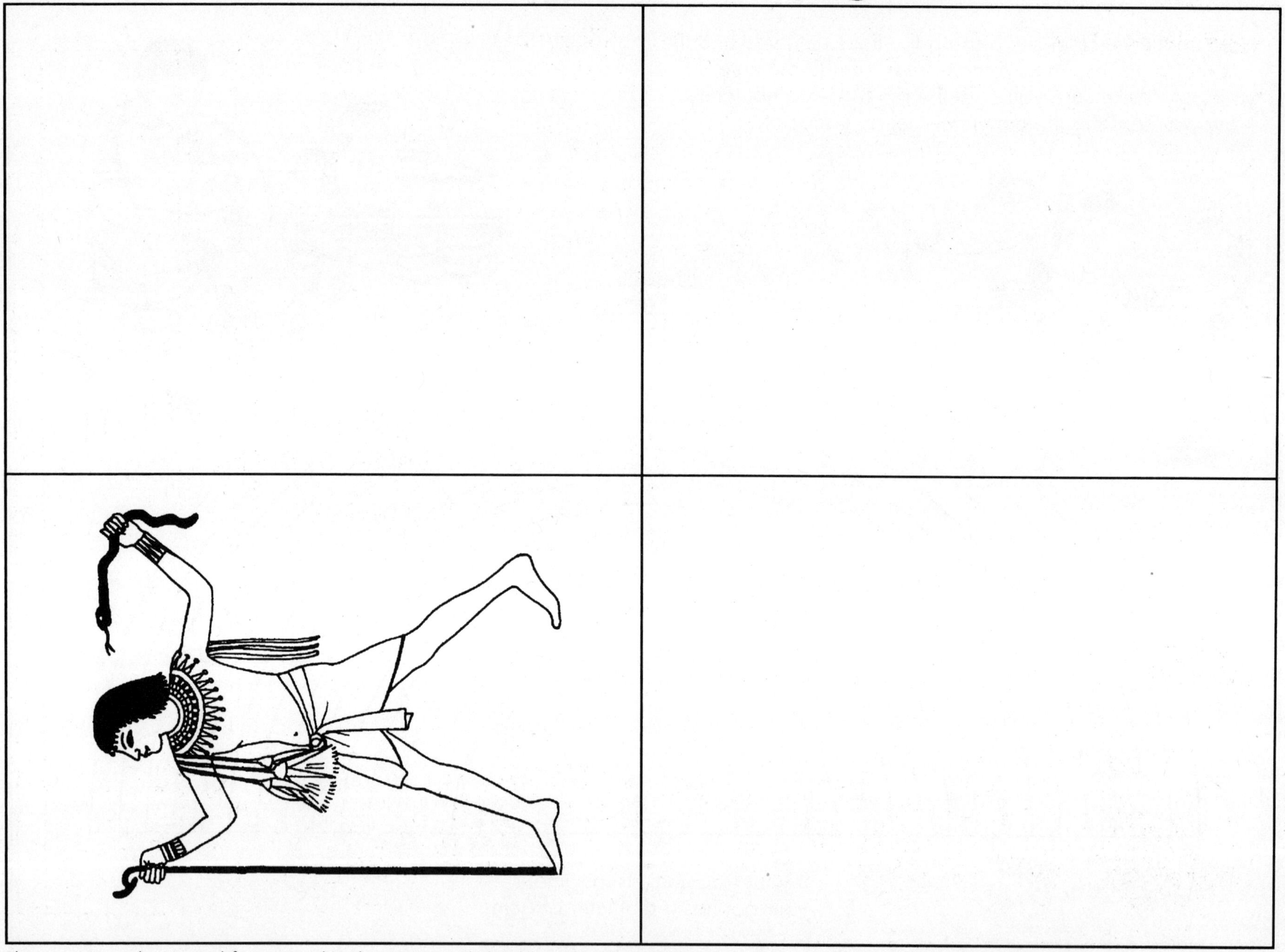

How to make a hat, see page 45

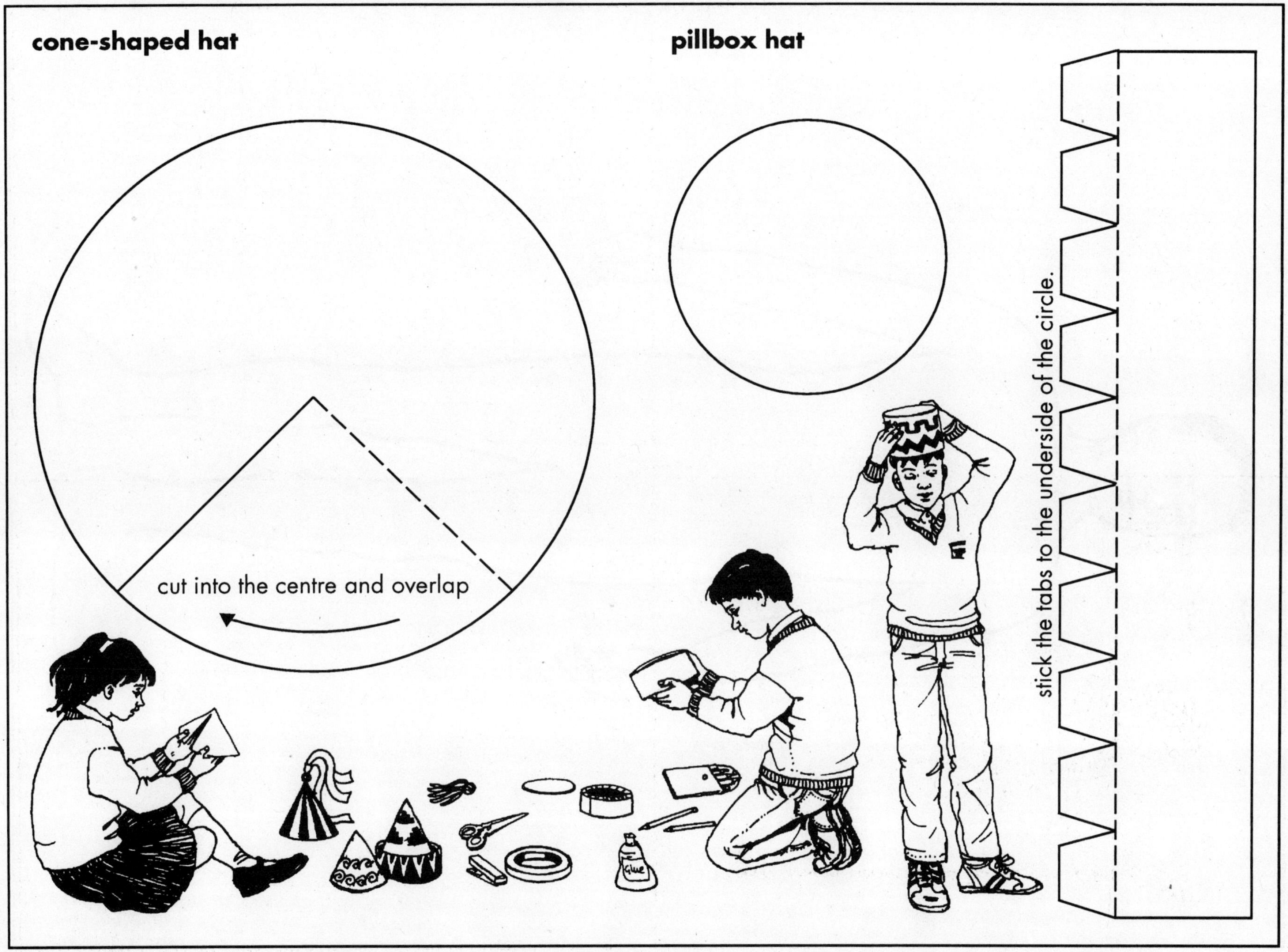

A male figure template, see pages 56 and 57

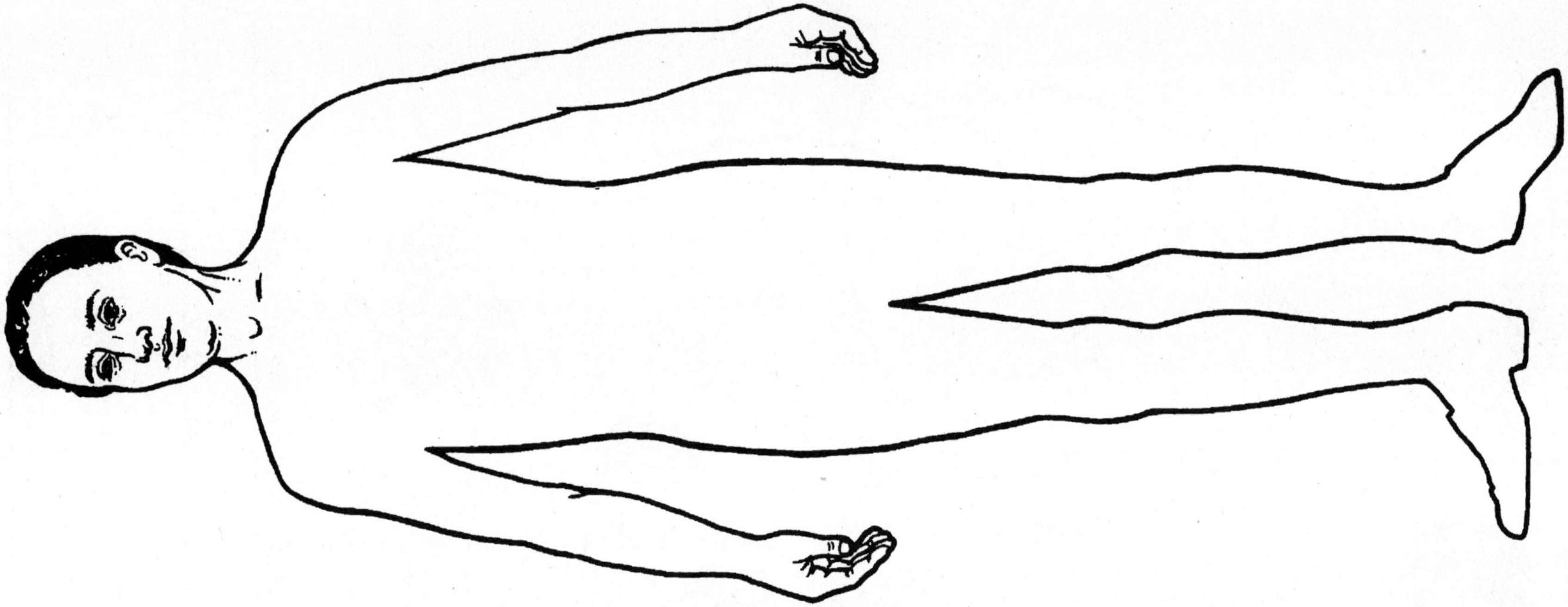

A female figure template, see pages 56 and 57

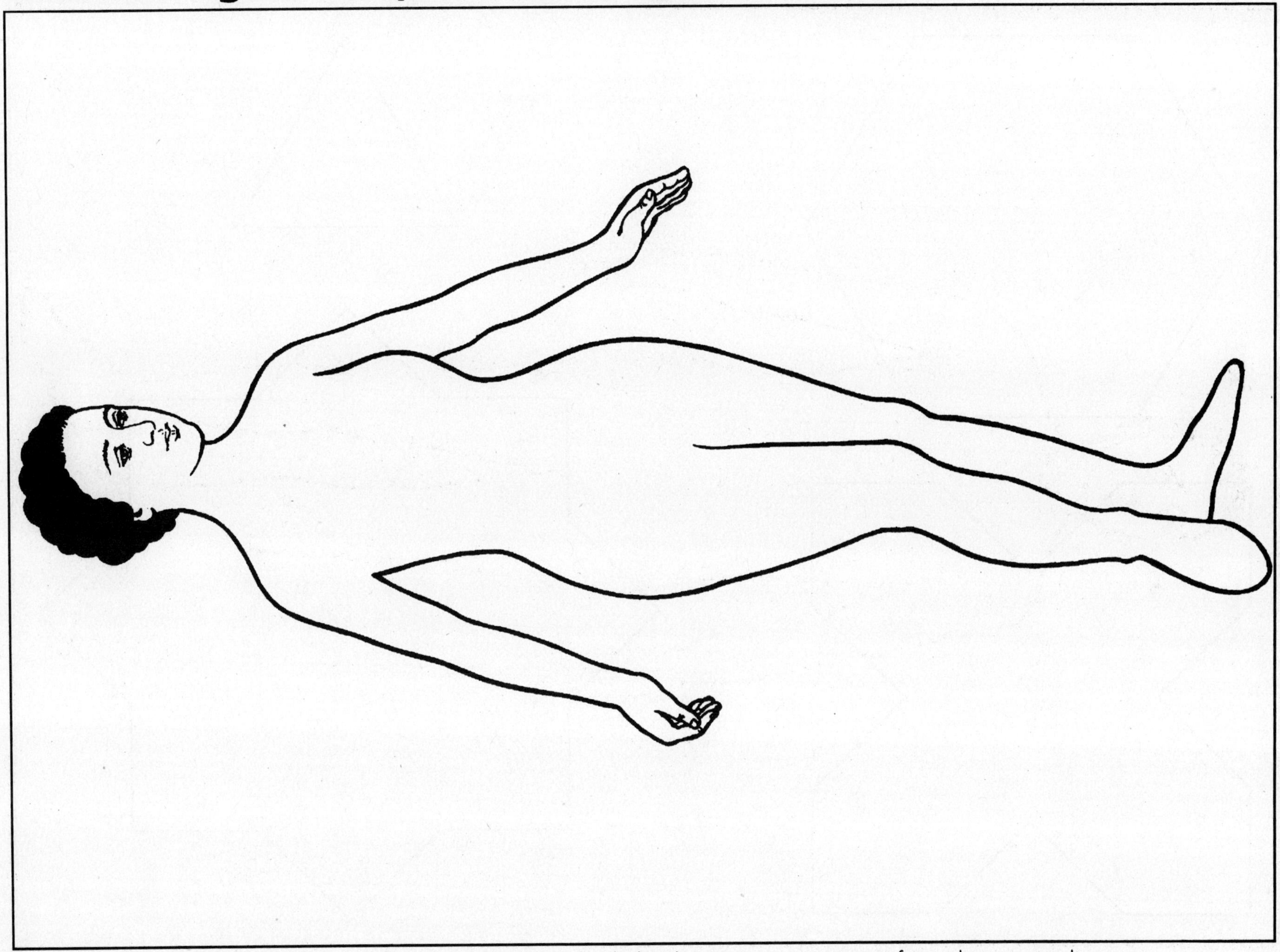

Shape templates, see page 83

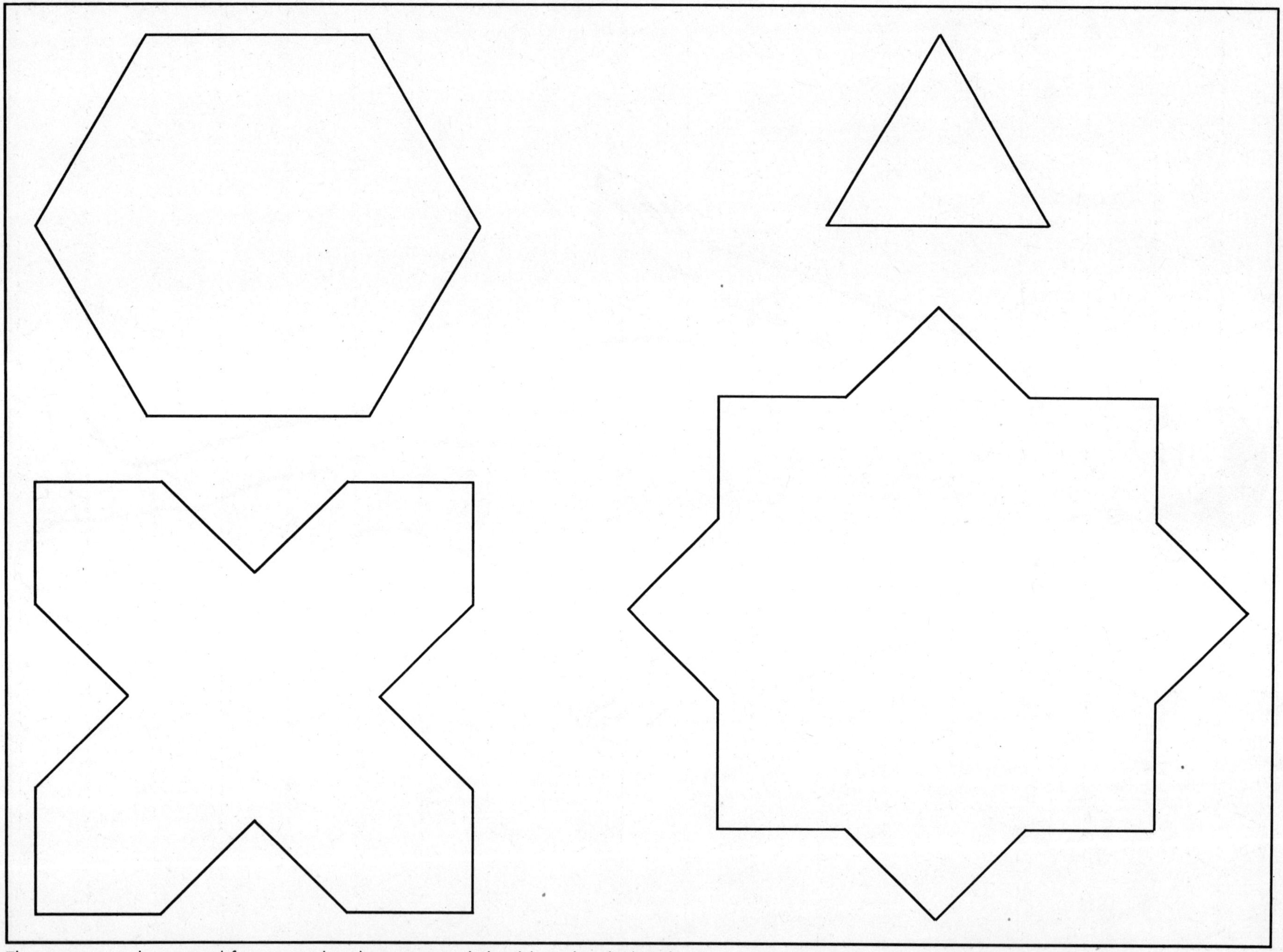

Isometric paper, see page 83

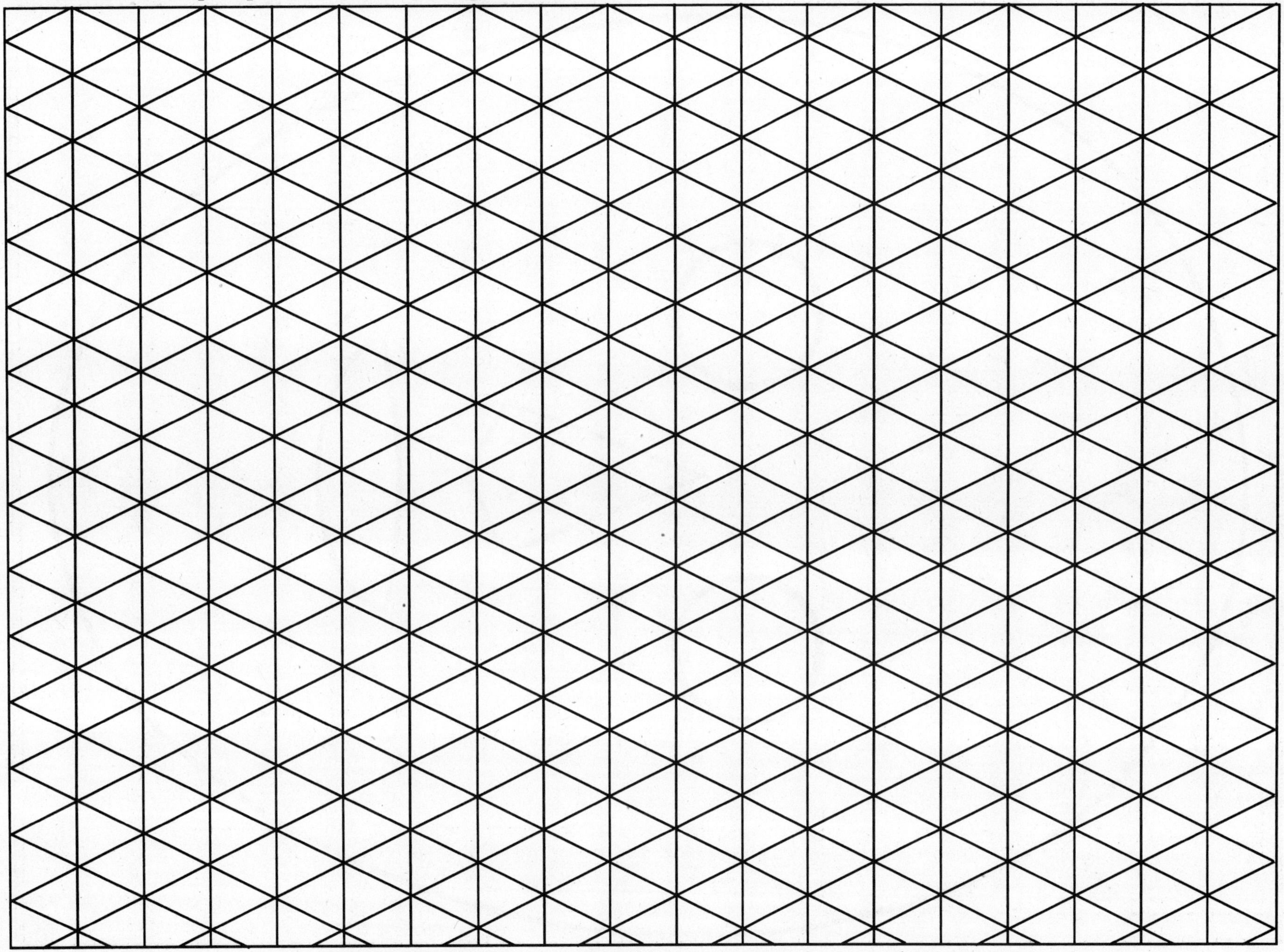

Mask 1, see page 86

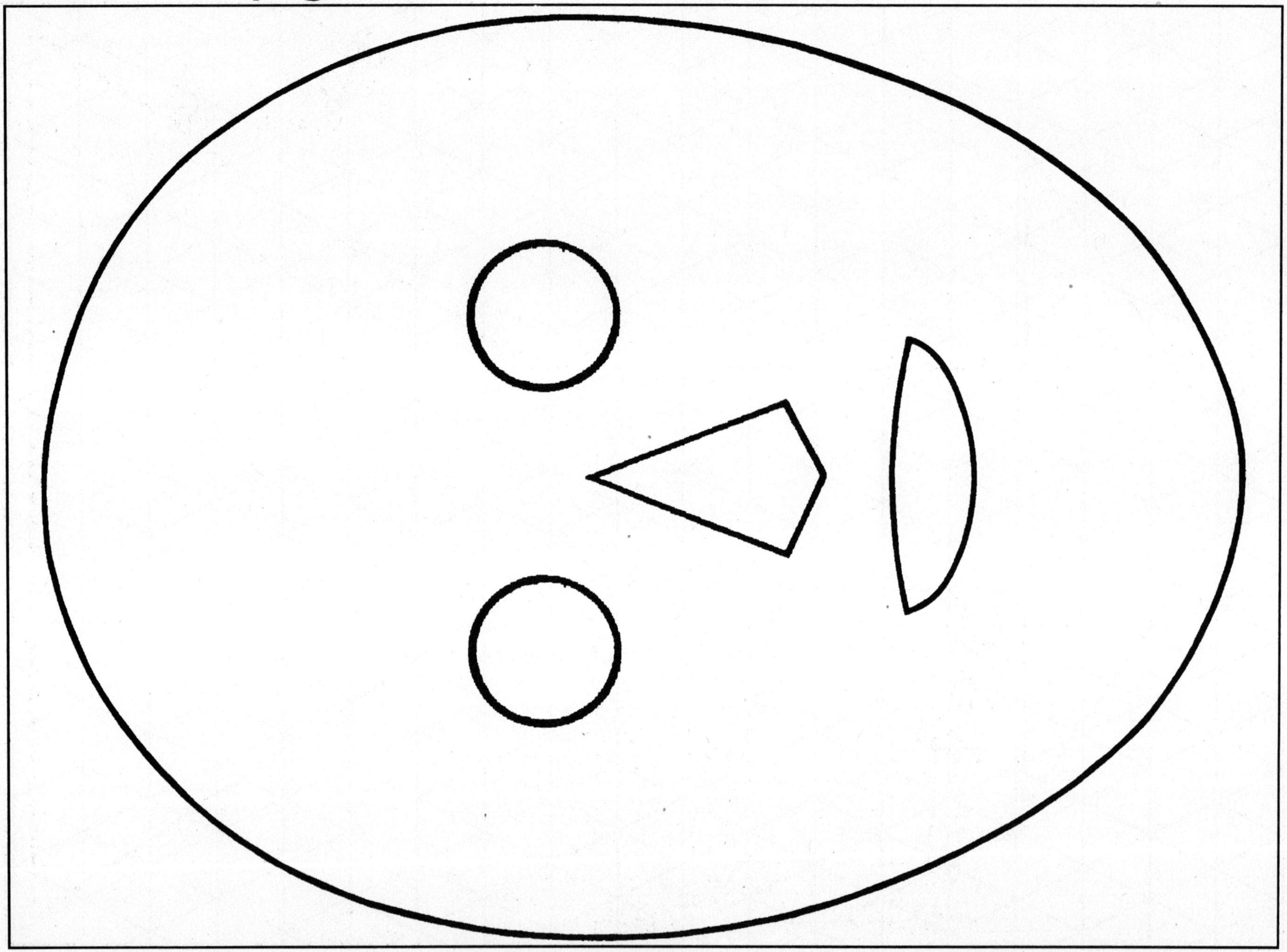

A weather vane kit, see page 93

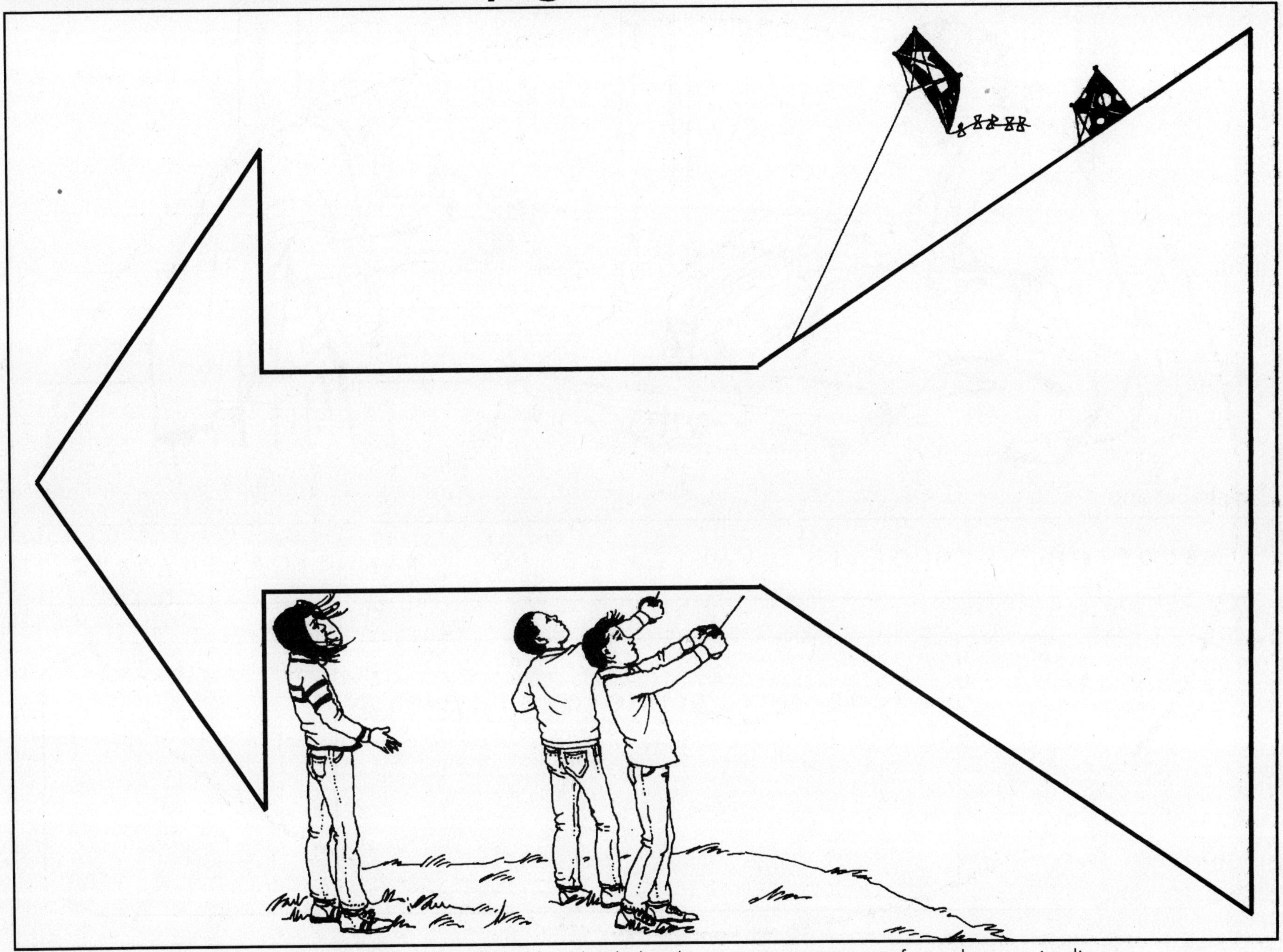

A secret code decipher, see page 96

alphabet strip

A B C D E F G H I J K L M N O P Q R S T U V W X Y Z A B C D E F G H I J K L M N O P Q R S T U V W X Y Z

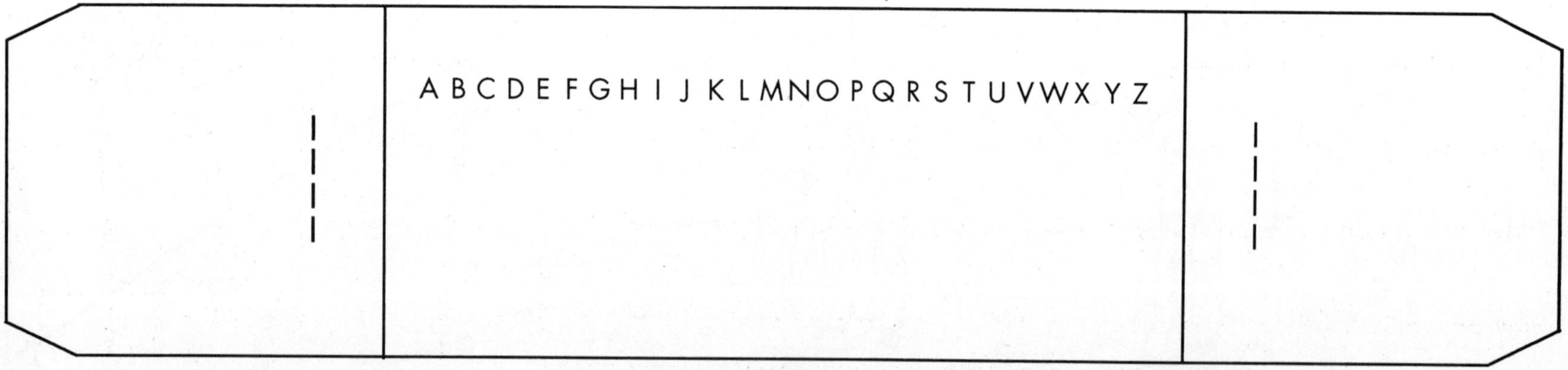

A visitor survey sheet, see page 103

Have you been to this museum before? ________

How many times? ________

Is there anything you were particularly wanting to see? ________

Do you plan to use the café? ________

Do you plan to buy or have you bought anything from the shop? ________

How did you travel here today? ________

How far have you travelled to come here today? ________

Are you staying away from home? ________

Are you on holiday? ________

Is this a day trip? ________

How many people did you come to the museum with? ________

How many women? How many men? How many children 16 or under?

________ women ________ men ________ children

A visitor travel survey sheet, see page 103

How far have the visitors travelled to get here?
Mark a dot to show how far.

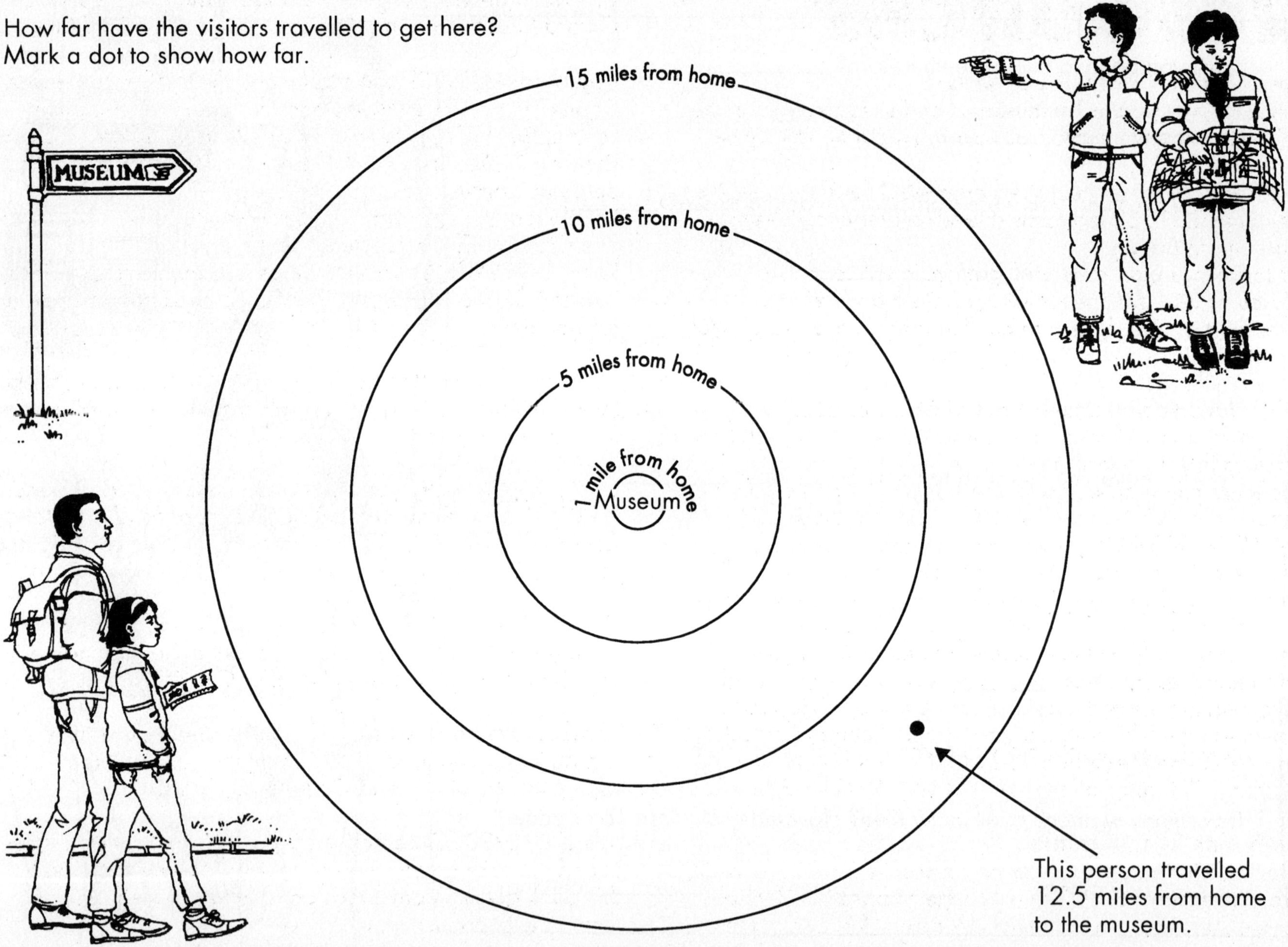

RESOURCES

Locating museums near you

The following guides list museums and sites throughout the UK. The reference section of your main public library is likely to hold them.

Exploring museums published by HMSO for the Museums Association, 1989 onwards. Eleven regional guides to museums in Britain.

Historic houses, castles and gardens open to the public and *Museums and galleries in Great Britain and Ireland* published by British Leisure Publications. These are annual directories (magazine format) available from shops like W H Smith.

Museums and galleries: a teacher's handbook G. Adams, published by Hutchinson. Lists museum and gallery education services in the London area.

The museums yearbook published annually by The Museums Association, 42 Clerkenwell Close, London ECIR OPA (tel. 0171-608 2933).

Resource list to support the implementation of National Curriculum History is published by the National Curriculum Council (Part 1 published March 1992, Part 2 April 1993). Part 2 especially includes references to museum collections and resources by Study Unit; however, it is not a complete compendium. Obtain copies from your local advisory teacher in the first instance, or from the School Curriculum and Assessment Authority (SCAA), Newcombe House, 45 Notting Hill Gate, London W11 3LQ (tel. 0171-229 1234).

Activities in museums

The English Heritage 'Education on site' series. The following are a selection from their vast range of books and videos for teachers. For full details and/or to order, contact the Education Service, English Heritage, Keysign House, 429 Oxford Street, London W1R 2HD (tel. 0171-973 3000).

Copeland, T. (1993) *Geography and the historic environment.*
Copeland,T. (1992) *Maths and the historic environment.*
Durbin, G. (1993) *A teacher's guide to using historic houses.*
Durbin, G., Morris, S., Wilkinson, S. (1992) *A teacher's guide to learning from objects.*
Fairclough, J. (1994) *History through role-play.*
Keen, J. (1995) *Ancient technology.*
Keith, C. (1991) *A teacher's guide to using listed buildings.*
Pownall, J. and Hutson, N. (1992) *Science and the historic environment.*

Heritage learning (the English Heritage magazine published by the Education Department) is distributed free to all schools in England every term.

Black, M., Brears, P., Corbishley, G., Renfrew, J. and Stead, J. (1993) *A taste of history: 10,000 years of food in Britain,* British Museum Press. Gives information about cooking and provides recipes from pre-history to the twentieth century.

Culpin, C. (1995) *Learning from country houses,* The National Trust. This explains the layout of country houses and the historical function of all the different rooms.

Newbery, E. and Fecher, S. (1994) *In the nick of time: a practical guide to teaching about the conservation of objects,* Museums and Galleries Commission.

West, J. (1990) *Classroom museum,* Elm Publications. If you intend to make a collection of objects for your classroom, this book gives helpful ideas on how to use them and tie them in with a museum visit.

Yorath, J. (1996) *Learning about science and technology in museums*, South Eastern Museums Service. This describes the way several schools have used museum collections to support their science and technology teaching.

Replica artefacts

The following companies supply catalogues of replica objects, documents and pictures for classroom use.
History in Evidence, Unit 4, Park Road, Holmewood, Chesterfield S42 5UY (tel. 01246 856363).
Articles of Antiquity and Articles of Faith, Bury Business Centre, Kay Street, Bury, Lancs BL9 6BU (tel. 0161 705 1878).

Pictures, postcards, posters, maps, etc.

These companies provide reproductions of the above. Send for their catalogues from:
The Goodwill Art Service, The Old School, Upton, Didcot, Oxfordshire OX11 9JB (tel. 01235 819598).
Historical Source Materials, Nicholas Roberts Publications, Long House, Church Road, Wisbech St Mary, Cambridgeshire PE13 4RN (tel. 01945 410648).
Shorewood Reproductions, Mainstone Publications, Sparham, Norwich NR9 5AQ (tel. 01362 688395).

Membership organisations

The following organisations provide meetings, training and publications for members and sometimes non-members. Contact them for details:

British Association for Local History, 24 Lower Street, Salisbury, Wiltshire SP2 8EY (tel. 01722 320155).
The Centre for Environmental Interpretation, Manchester Metropolitan University, St Augustines, Lower Chatham Street, Manchester M15 6BY (tel. 0161-247 1067).
The Group for Education in Museums, The Membership Secretary, 16 Somerset Gardens, Teddington TW11 8TA (tel. 0171-735 3699).
The Historical Association, 59a Kennington Park Road, London SE11 (tel. 0171-735 3901).

Useful books

Earl, A. and Sensier, D (1994) *Traditions around the world*, Wayland (Publishers) Ltd.
McIntosh, J. (1994) *Eyewitness guides: archaeology*, Dorling Kindersley.
Morley, J. (1992) *Timelines clothes for work, play and display*, Watts.
Talboys, G. (1996) *Using museums as an educational resource arena*, Ashgate Publishing Limited.